Cheap Eats

THE AUSTRALIAN
Women's Weekly

contents

What fun this book was to develop! It didn't take us any time at all to come up with its content: in fact, we had to pick and choose our selection from a wealth of cheap and very cheerful recipe suggestions. People who love food and love to cook have always known that it's not necessary to spend a motser on ingredients to create a gobsmackingly awesome meal, and this delightful compilation of ideas deliciously and simply proves the point. Enjoy.

Pamela Clark

Food Director

cheap chic

Cheap food doesn't have to mean bad food. Some of the most popular dishes from every country around the world, so-called peasant food, cost next-to-nothing to prepare: confirmation that it's possible to make an appetising dish with affordable ingredients. Whether you have a family of five to feed, or you're a student on a tight budget, and you feel like you're spending more on groceries than you like (or than you need), the recipes in this book, and the ideas you gather from our hints, will help ensure you eat healthily, cook wisely and enjoy the food in the process. Forward planning is one of the keys to eating on a budget. If you find yourself scratching around the pantry when you come home from work searching for inspiration, and you're starving, the temptation for the quick-fix – pre-made from the supermarket, takeaway or home-delivered – can be irresistible. But it's an expensive choice to make, health-wise and financially. And, really, it's just as easy, given some thoughtful deliberation and a dollop of nous, to make your own

meals at home, no cryovac-packed mains from the deli, no takeaway, and this cookbook proves it. You can create fine food without breaking the budget. There's not much rocket science involved: start by planning a list of meals for the week, combine it with keen motivation, sensible shopping and exciting recipe suggestions, and you'll come up with a viable game plan that sees delicious and healthy food on the table without blowing the budget or requiring a lot of time and a great deal of effort to prepare. And, if you add to the equation a little interest in and love for cooking, you'll find the whole experience is no longer something you dread, but an opportunity to try myriad ideas that delight the tastebuds without emptying the wallet.

to market, to market

Always take a written shopping list and several menu ideas with you to the supermarket and, if at all possible, don't shop when you're hungry. Resist the impulse buy: if it's not on the list

loading the larder

First-class ingredients don't necessarily have to come with a hefty price-tag. Shop around and buy staples when they're priced well (always check the "use-by" date). Use the list below to help keep the pantry in ready-set-go mode to avoid frustration when you settle in to cook.

5

it doesn't go in the trolley. Don't be distracted by gimmicks, but do note special offers if they're a product on your list; buy in bulk and stock up on non-perishables when they are on special.

Compare prices between supermarkets; don't be afraid to buy generic brands, but remember that the range and quality of goods between stores does vary.

Buy fruit and vegetables that are in-season, and frequent a greengrocer that reduces its remaining produce prices at the end of the day. Some supermarkets, too, offer fantastic markdowns on items like bread, meat and dairy goods as they near their use-by dates. Divide the meat into 250g portions and freeze it, or cook it all at once to make a mega-quantity of one recipe then freeze that in meal-sized servings. Don't be afraid of cooking in bulk: thawing a curry or stew on a night when you're too tired to cook is almost as much of a treat as eating out. Recycle leftovers in different delicious guises. Get creative in the kitchen – cheap eats shouldn't have to be synonymous with stingy or second-rate sustenance.

plain flour
cornflour
bicarbonate of soda
white, caster and brown sugars
salt and black pepper
vegetable and olive oils
long and short pastas
cereals and grains
white, brown, arborio and basmati rices
canned and dried beans
dried lentils and chickpeas
tomato sauce
mayonnaise
french and wholegrain mustards
balsamic, red and white wine vinegars
worcestershire sauce
light, dark and sweet soy sauce
canned tomatoes
canned soups
canned fruits
canned tuna and salmon
tetra packs of stocks
dried herbs and spices
indian and thai curry pastes
teas, herbal and ordinary
coffee, instant and beans
nuts and dried fruits
jams and marmalades
chutneys
potatoes
onions
garlic

tuna spinach mornay pie with mash

50g butter
1 medium brown onion (150g), sliced thinly
¼ cup (35g) plain flour
2 cups (500ml) milk, warmed
150g baby spinach leaves
425g can tuna in springwater, drained
2 tablespoons lemon juice
potato and celeriac mash
400g potatoes, chopped coarsely
300g celeriac, chopped coarsely
2 tablespoons milk
30g butter
¼ cup (20g) finely grated parmesan cheese

1 Make potato and celeriac mash.
2 Melt butter in medium saucepan; cook onion, stirring, about 5 minutes or until softened. Add flour; cook, stirring, until mixture thickens and bubbles. Gradually add milk; stir until mixture boils and thickens. Remove from heat; stir in spinach, tuna and juice.
3 Preheat grill.
4 Spoon tuna mixture into shallow flameproof 1.5 litre (6-cup) dish; top with mash. Grill until browned lightly.
potato and celeriac mash Boil, steam or microwave potato and celeriac, separately, until tender; drain. Combine potato and celeriac in large bowl; mash with milk and butter until smooth. Stir in cheese; cover to keep warm.

preparation time **20 minutes**
cooking time **30 minutes** serves **4**
per serving 25.8g total fat (12.1g saturated fat); 2040kJ (488 cal); 29.7g carbohydrate; 31.7g protein; 5.8g fibre

salmon and green bean potato patties

150g green beans
800g potatoes, chopped coarsely
20g butter
⅓ cup (25g) finely grated parmesan cheese
1 egg
415g can red salmon
⅓ cup (35g) packaged breadcrumbs
vegetable oil, for shallow-frying
150g baby spinach leaves
1 medium lemon (140g), cut into wedges

1 Boil, steam or microwave beans until tender; drain. Rinse under cold water; drain. Chop coarsely.
2 Boil, steam or microwave potatoe until tender; drain. Mash potato in large bowl with butter, cheese and egg until smooth.
3 Drain salmon; discard skin and bones. Add salmon and beans to potato mixture; mix well. Shape salmon mixture into 12 patties; coat in breadcrumbs. Place patties on tray, cover; refrigerate 30 minutes.
4 Heat oil in large frying pan; shallow-fry patties, in batches, until browned lightly and heated through. Drain on absorbent paper; serve on baby spinach with lemon wedges.

preparation time **20 minutes** (plus refrigeration time)
cooking time **30 minutes** serves **4**
per serving **51.7g** total fat (**8.7g** saturated fat); **2959kJ** (**708 cal**); **29.6g** carbohydrate; **29.5g** protein; **5.6g** fibre

We used sebago potatoes in this recipe; you can also use lasoda, coliban, nicola or pink-eye.

lemon, coconut and chilli poached fish

You can use any firm white fish fillet, such as ling, perch or blue eye, in this recipe.

1½ cups (300g) jasmine rice
400ml can coconut cream
2 tablespoons fish sauce
1 tablespoon finely grated lemon rind
¼ cup (60ml) lemon juice
2 fresh long red chillies, chopped finely
3cm piece fresh ginger (15g), grated
4 x 200g firm white fish fillets
¼ cup fresh coriander leaves

1 Cook rice in large saucepan of boiling water, uncovered, until just tender; drain.
2 Meanwhile, combine coconut cream, sauce, rind, juice, chilli and ginger in medium frying pan; bring to a boil. Reduce heat; simmer, uncovered, 10 minutes. Add fish; simmer, covered, about 10 minutes or until cooked as desired. Remove from heat; stir in coriander.
3 Top rice with fish, drizzle with coconut cream sauce.

preparation time **15 minutes**
cooking time **25 minutes** serves **4**
per serving 26.8g total fat (20.4g saturated fat); 2955kJ (707 cal); 64.4g carbohydrate; 49.6g protein; 4g fibre

clam chowder

If clams are not available, replace them with either vongole or pipis.

1kg baby clams
2 tablespoons coarse cooking salt
40g butter
1 large brown onion (200g), chopped coarsely
2 rindless bacon rashers (130g), chopped coarsely
1 clove garlic, crushed
2 tablespoons plain flour
3 cups (750ml) milk, warmed
2 cups (500ml) vegetable stock, warmed
2 medium potatoes (400g), chopped coarsely
2 tablespoons finely chopped fresh chives

1 Rinse clams under cold water; place in large bowl, sprinkle with salt, cover with water. Stand 1 hour; rinse, drain.
2 Meanwhile, melt butter in large saucepan; cook onion, bacon and garlic, stirring, until onion softens. Add flour to pan; cook, stirring, until mixture thickens and bubbles. Gradually stir in milk and stock; stir until mixture boils and thickens slightly. Add potato, reduce heat; simmer, covered, until potato is tender.
3 Add clams; simmer, covered, about 5 minutes or until clams open (discard any that do not). Remove from heat; stir in chives. Serve chowder with grilled slices of french bread, if desired.

preparation time **15 minutes** (plus standing time)
cooking time **25 minutes** serves **4**
per serving 19.4g total fat (8.8g saturated fat); 1672kJ (400 cal); 28.7g carbohydrate; 26.4g protein; 2.5g fibre

chicken

12

citrus chicken with vermicelli salad

¼ cup (60ml) lemon juice
2 fresh small red thai chillies, sliced thinly
¼ cup (85g) orange marmalade
2 cloves garlic, crushed
4 chicken marylands (1.4kg)
250g rice vermicelli
2 medium oranges (480g)
⅔ cup loosely packed fresh mint leaves
1 medium lebanese cucumber (130g),
    seeded, sliced thinly crossways
citrus dressing
2 tablespoons lemon juice
2 tablespoons orange marmalade
2 teaspoons vegetable oil

1 Combine juice, chilli, marmalade and garlic in large bowl. Pierce chicken all over with skewer; add to bowl. Turn to coat in marinade. Cover; refrigerate 3 hours or overnight.

2 Preheat oven to 200°C/180°C fan-forced.

3 Place drained chicken on oiled wire rack in large shallow baking dish; reserve marinade. Roast, uncovered, about 45 minutes or until cooked through, brushing occasionally with reserved marinade.

4 Meanwhile, place vermicelli in large heatproof bowl, cover with boiling water. Stand until just tender; drain. Rinse vermicelli under cold water; drain. Using scissors, cut vermicelli into random lengths.

5 Segment orange over small bowl; reserve 2 teaspoons of juice.

6 Make citrus dressing.

7 Combine vermicelli and orange segments in large bowl with mint, cucumber and dressing; toss gently. Serve salad with chicken.

citrus dressing Place ingredients and reserved orange juice in screw-top jar; shake well.

preparation time **15 minutes (plus refrigeration time)**
cooking time **45 minutes** serves **4**
per serving **36.1g total fat (10.9g saturated fat); 3520kJ (842 cal); 75g carbohydrate; 51.1g protein; 4.8g fibre**

caramelised chicken cutlets

2 teaspoons vegetable oil
4 chicken thigh cutlets (800g), skin on
1 medium red onion (170g), sliced thinly
3 cloves garlic, sliced thinly
¼ cup (55g) brown sugar
1 tablespoon dark soy sauce
1 tablespoon fish sauce
⅓ cup coarsely chopped fresh coriander

1 Preheat oven to 200°C/180°C fan-forced.
2 Heat oil in large frying pan; cook chicken, both sides, until browned. Place chicken, in single layer, in baking dish. Roast chicken, uncovered, in oven, about 25 minutes or until cooked through.
3 Meanwhile, heat same frying pan; cook onion and garlic, stirring, until onion softens. Add sugar and sauces; cook, stirring, 3 minutes. Return chicken to pan with coriander; turn chicken to coat in mixture.

preparation time **20 minutes**
cooking time **35 minutes** serves **4**
per serving 22.4g total fat (6.9g saturated fat); 1538kJ (368 cal); 16.3g carbohydrate; 24.8g protein; 1g fibre

mexican chicken stew

1 tablespoon vegetable oil
8 chicken drumsticks (1.2kg)
1 large red onion (300g), sliced thickly
2 cloves garlic, crushed
2 fresh long red chillies, chopped finely
1 teaspoon ground cumin
4 medium tomatoes (600g), chopped coarsely
1 cup (250ml) chicken stock
⅓ cup loosely packed fresh oregano leaves
420g can kidney beans, rinsed, drained
1 medium yellow capsicum (200g),
    sliced thickly
1 medium green capsicum (200g),
    sliced thickly

1 Heat half the oil in large saucepan; cook chicken, in batches, until browned all over. Heat remaining oil in pan; cook onion, garlic, chilli and cumin, stirring, until onion softens.
2 Return chicken to pan with tomato, stock and ¼ cup of the oregano; bring to a boil. Reduce heat; simmer, covered, 30 minutes.
3 Add beans and capsicums; simmer, uncovered, 20 minutes. Divide stew among bowls; sprinkle with remaining oregano. Serve with sour cream, if desired.

preparation time **20 minutes**
cooking time **1 hour** serves **4**
per serving 26.5g total fat (7.1g saturated fat); 2090kJ (500 cal); 19g carbohydrate; 42.6g protein; 8.4g fibre

You need to purchase a large barbecued chicken weighing approximately 900g for this recipe.

chicken, leek and mushroom pies

1 tablespoon vegetable oil
1 medium leek (350g), sliced thinly
2 rindless bacon rashers (130g), sliced thinly
200g mushrooms, halved
1 tablespoon plain flour
1 cup (250ml) chicken stock
⅓ cup (80ml) cream
1 tablespoon dijon mustard
3 cups (480g) coarsely chopped
    barbecued chicken
1 sheet ready-rolled puff pastry, quartered

1 Preheat oven to 200°C/180°C fan-forced.
2 Heat oil in medium saucepan; cook leek, bacon and mushrooms, stirring, until leek softens. Stir in flour; cook, stirring, until mixture thickens and bubbles. Gradually add stock; cook, stirring, until mixture boils and thickens. Stir in cream, mustard and chicken.
3 Divide mixture among four 1-cup (250ml) ovenproof dishes; top each with a pastry quarter. Bake, uncovered, in oven, about 20 minutes or until browned.

preparation time 15 minutes
cooking time 45 minutes serves 4
per serving 44.7g total fat (13.1g saturated fat); 2780kJ (665 cal); 20.4g carbohydrate; 44.5g protein; 3.7g fibre

cost-cutter Buy a few barbecued chickens when they're on special, remove and shred the meat then freeze it in one-cup parcels – ready for use at another time, and effectively saving time and money. Discard the chicken skin, but use the bones, along with any slightly worse-for-wear carrots, celery or herbs in your vegetable crisper, to make stock and freeze it in 1-cup amounts.

meat

chinese barbecued spareribs

¾ cup (180ml) barbecue sauce
2 tablespoons dark soy sauce
1 tablespoon honey
¼ cup (60ml) orange juice
2 tablespoons brown sugar
1 clove garlic, crushed
2cm piece fresh ginger (10g), grated
2kg slabs american-style pork spareribs

1 Combine sauces, honey, juice, sugar, garlic and ginger in large shallow dish; add ribs, turn to coat in marinade. Cover; refrigerate 3 hours or overnight.
2 Preheat oven to 180°C/160°C fan-forced.
3 Brush ribs both sides with marinade; place, in single layer, in large shallow baking dish; roast, covered, 45 minutes. Uncover; roast about 15 minutes or until ribs are browned. Serve with fried rice, if desired.

preparation time **15 minutes (plus refrigeration time)**
cooking time **1 hour** serves **4**
per serving **26.4g** total fat (**10.2g** saturated fat); **2675kJ** (**640 cal**); **35.2g** carbohydrate; **64.7g** protein; **0.8g** fibre

Ask your butcher to cut pork spareribs "american-style" for this recipe. These will be slabs of 8 to 10 ribs, cut from the mid-loin, with almost all of the fat removed.

caramelised corned beef with sweet mustard sauce

1.5kg piece corned silverside
2 dried bay leaves
1 medium brown onion (150g),
    chopped coarsely
½ cup (125ml) red wine vinegar
¾ cup (165g) firmly packed brown sugar
8 baby new potatoes (320g), halved
2 medium carrots (240g),
    quartered lengthways
80g butter
8 pickling onions (320g), halved
2 medium zucchini (240g),
    quartered lengthways
2 teaspoons fresh thyme leaves
1 tablespoon plain flour
1 tablespoon wholegrain mustard

1 Cover beef, bay leaves, brown onion, half the vinegar and a third of the brown sugar with cold water in large saucepan; bring to a boil. Reduce heat; simmer, uncovered, about 1½ hours or until beef is tender. Remove from heat; stand, covered, 30 minutes.
2 Meanwhile, boil, steam or microwave potato and carrot, separately, until almost tender. Drain; cover to keep warm.
3 Drain beef over medium bowl; reserve 2 cups cooking liquid, discard remaining liquid and solids.
4 Melt butter in same cleaned pan; cook pickling onion, stirring, until softened. Stir in remaining vinegar and brown sugar. Add potato, carrot, zucchini and thyme; cook, stirring, until vegetables are caramelised. Transfer vegetables to serving dish; cover to keep warm.
5 Return beef to pan; cook, turning, about 5 minutes or until caramelised. Remove beef; stand, covered, 5 minutes then slice thinly.
6 Meanwhile, add flour to same pan; cook, stirring, until mixture thickens and bubbles. Add mustard then reserved cooking liquid; stir until mixture boils and thickens slightly. Serve beef and vegetables drizzled with mustard sauce.

preparation time **20 minutes**
cooking time **2 hours (plus standing time)** serves **4**
per serving 28.8g total fat (4.5g saturated fat); 3357kJ (803 cal); 62.3g carbohydrate; 70g protein; 5.9g fibre

balti beef curry

1 tablespoon vegetable oil
750g beef skirt steak, cut into 2cm dice
1 clove garlic, crushed
1 medium brown onion (150g),
    chopped coarsely
2cm piece fresh ginger (10g), grated
½ cup (150g) balti curry paste
410g can crushed tomatoes
¾ cup (180ml) water
½ cup (125ml) buttermilk
½ cup coarsely chopped fresh
    coriander leaves
1 medium tomato (150g), seeded,
    sliced thinly

1 Heat half the oil in large deep frying pan;
cook beef, in batches, until browned all over.
2 Heat remaining oil in pan; cook garlic,
onion and ginger, stirring, until onion softens.
Add curry paste; cook, stirring, until paste is
blended with onion mixture.
3 Return beef to pan with undrained tomatoes
and the water; bring to a boil. Reduce heat;
simmer, covered, 45 minutes. Uncover; simmer
about 10 minutes or until beef is tender,
stirring occasionally. Remove from heat; stir
in buttermilk. Sprinkle curry with coriander
and tomato, and serve with steamed basmati
rice, if desired.

preparation time **10 minutes**
cooking time **1 hour 10 minutes** serves **4**
per serving **21.8g total fat (4.1g saturated fat); 1839kJ
(440 cal); 10.7g carbohydrate; 47.3g protein; 6.2g fibre**

beef and onion casserole

1kg beef chuck steak, cut into 2cm dice
⅓ cup (50g) plain flour
2 tablespoons olive oil
2 small brown onions (200g),
    chopped coarsely
2 cloves garlic, crushed
150g mushrooms, quartered
1 cup (250ml) dry red wine
400g can crushed tomatoes
2 cups (500ml) beef stock
2 tablespoons tomato paste

1 Coat beef in flour, shake away excess.
Heat half the oil in large saucepan; cook
beef, in batches, until browned all over. Heat
remaining oil in same pan; cook onion, garlic
and mushrooms, stirring, until onion softens.
2 Return beef to pan with wine, undrained
tomatoes, stock and paste; bring to a boil.
Reduce heat; simmer, covered, 40 minutes.
Uncover; simmer about 40 minutes or until
meat is tender and sauce thickens slightly,
stirring occasionally.

preparation time **20 minutes**
cooking time **1 hour 30 minutes** serves **4**
per serving **21.2g total fat (6.2g saturated fat); 2245kJ
(537 cal); 17.4g carbohydrate; 56.8g protein; 4g fibre**

cost-cutter Also called black-eyed peas or cow peas, dried black-eyed beans are found in most supermarkets and large greengrocers alongside a wide range of other pulses, any of which can be substituted for what we've used here. Dried beans, peas, split peas and lentils are wise selections for the cook on a budget: not only are they cheap and filling, but are a good source of non-meat protein.

pork and black-eyed beans

1 cup (200g) black-eyed beans
1kg pork neck, sliced thickly
⅓ cup (50g) plain flour
2 tablespoons olive oil
1 medium brown onion (150g),
    chopped coarsely
2 cloves garlic, crushed
½ teaspoon five-spice powder
1 teaspoon sichuan peppercorns,
    crushed coarsely
½ teaspoon chilli powder
½ cup (125ml) dry white wine
3 cups (750ml) chicken stock
2 teaspoons finely grated orange rind
½ cup coarsely chopped fresh flat-leaf parsley

1 Place beans in medium bowl, cover with cold water; stand overnight, drain. Rinse under cold water; drain.
2 Coat pork in flour, shake away excess. Heat half the oil in large flameproof casserole dish; cook pork, in batches, until browned all over.
3 Heat remaining oil in same dish; cook onion, garlic, five-spice, pepper and chilli, stirring, until spices are fragrant and onion softens. Add beans, wine and stock; bring to a boil.
4 Return pork to dish; simmer, covered, 40 minutes. Uncover; simmer about 30 minutes or until pork is tender and sauce thickens slightly, stirring occasionally. Remove from heat; stir in rind and parsley.

preparation time **20 minutes (plus standing time)**
cooking time **1 hour 30 minutes** serves **4**
per serving **19.9g total fat (5.1g saturated fat); 2608kJ (624 cal); 30.3g carbohydrate; 71.4g protein; 8.5g fibre**

You need 1kg of untrimmed silver beet to get the amount of trimmed silver beet required for this recipe.

lamb and barley soup

1.5kg french-trimmed lamb shanks
3 litres (12 cups) water
¾ cup (150g) pearl barley
1 medium carrot (120g), sliced thinly
1 medium leek (350g), sliced thinly
2 trimmed celery stalks (200g), sliced thinly
1 tablespoon curry powder
250g trimmed silver beet, chopped coarsely

1 Combine lamb, the water and barley in large saucepan; bring to a boil. Reduce heat; simmer, uncovered, 1 hour, skimming surface and stirring occasionally. Add carrot, leek and celery; simmer, uncovered, 10 minutes.

2 Remove lamb from soup mixture. When cool enough to handle, remove meat; chop coarsely. Discard bones and any fat or skin.

3 Dry-fry curry powder in small saucepan until fragrant. Return meat to soup with curry powder and silver beet; cook, uncovered, until silver beet wilts.

preparation time **15 minutes**
cooking time **1 hour 25 minutes serves 6**
per serving **13.3g total fat (5.7g saturated fat); 1404kJ (336 cal); 18.9g carbohydrate; 31.8g protein; 6.4g fibre**

cost-cutter Think about using lamb shanks that have not been french-trimmed or use 2kg lamb neck chops in this soup. The money saved will more than make up for any extra effort expended trimming excess fat from the meat before you cook it or skimming fat off the soup's surface.

pork sausages with grilled polenta and spicy tomato sauce

1 litre (4 cups) water
1 cup (170g) polenta
1 cup (120g) coarsely grated cheddar cheese
2 teaspoons olive oil
1 medium red onion (170g), sliced thinly
1 clove garlic, crushed
1 fresh small red thai chilli, chopped finely
4 medium tomatoes (600g), chopped coarsely
8 thick pork sausages (960g)

1 Bring the water to a boil in medium saucepan; gradually stir in polenta. Reduce heat; simmer, stirring, until polenta thickens. Stir in cheese. Spread polenta into oiled deep 19cm-square cake pan, cover; refrigerate about 1 hour or until polenta firms.
2 Meanwhile, heat oil in medium saucepan; cook onion, garlic and chilli, stirring, until onion softens. Add tomato; simmer, covered, until tomato softens.
3 Cut polenta into quarters. Cook polenta and sausages, in batches, on heated oiled grill plate (or grill or barbecue) until polenta is browned both sides and sausages are cooked through.
4 Serve sausages on polenta squares, topped with spicy tomato sauce. Serve sprinkled with fresh thyme leaves, if desired.

preparation time **20 minutes** cooking time **15 minutes (plus refrigeration time)** serves 4
per serving **65.6g total fat (28.3g saturated fat); 3908kJ (935 cal); 42.2g carbohydrate; 42g protein; 6.8g fibre**

curried sausages

800g thick beef sausages
20g butter
1 medium brown onion (150g),
    chopped coarsely
1 tablespoon curry powder
2 teaspoons plain flour
2 large carrots (360g), chopped coarsely
2 trimmed celery stalks (200g),
    chopped coarsely
500g baby new potatoes, halved
2 cups (500ml) beef stock
1 cup loosely packed fresh
    flat-leaf parsley leaves

1 Cook sausages, in batches, in heated deep large frying pan until cooked through. Cut each sausage into thirds.
2 Melt butter in same cleaned pan; cook onion, stirring, until soft. Add curry powder and flour; cook, stirring, 2 minutes.
3 Add vegetables and stock; bring to a boil. Reduce heat; simmer, covered, about 15 minutes or until vegetables are tender. Add sausages; simmer, uncovered, until sauce thickens slightly. Stir in parsley.

preparation time **20 minutes**
cooking time **45 minutes** serves 4
per serving **55.8g total fat (27.3g saturated fat); 3177kJ (760 cal); 29.8g carbohydrate; 30.1g protein; 12.8g fibre**

Store leftover bolognese, covered, in the refrigerator for up to 3 days or in the freezer for up to 3 months.

spaghetti bolognese

1 tablespoon olive oil
2 large brown onions (400g), chopped finely
4 cloves garlic, crushed
1.2kg beef mince
2 large carrots (360g), grated coarsely
⅓ cup (95g) tomato paste
3 cups (750ml) beef stock
2 x 810g cans crushed tomatoes
1 tablespoon mixed dried herbs
500g spaghetti

1   Heat oil in large saucepan; cook onion and garlic, stirring, until onion softens.
2   Add mince; cook, stirring, until browned. Add carrot and tomato paste; cook, stirring, 5 minutes. Add stock, undrained tomato and herbs; bring to a boil. Reduce heat; simmer, covered, 45 minutes, stirring occasionally. Uncover; simmer, about 45 minutes or until thickened slightly.
3   About 10 minutes before sauce is ready, cook pasta in large saucepan of boiling water, uncovered, until just tender; drain.
4   Serve half the bolognese with spaghetti, reserve remaining half of bolognese for another use (see page 84 for ideas). Serve with grated parmesan, if desired.

preparation time **15 minutes**
cooking time **1 hour 40 minutes** serves **4**
per serving **39.8g total fat (15.2g saturated fat); 4836kJ (1157 cal); 110g carbohydrate; 81.8g protein; 13.7g fibre**

cost-cutter In late summer, when tomatoes are in abundance, greengrocers often sell boxes of the overripe or damaged fruit at next to nothing. If you cook these down (peeled is nice, but not necessary), they are both cheaper and better to use than their canned counterparts. The cooked tomato can be sieved, pureed or left as is and added to the mince mixture for this sauce.

pasta

32

pea and salmon pasta bake

375g rigatoni pasta
40g butter
2 tablespoons plain flour
2 cups (500ml) milk
1½ cups (180g) frozen peas
½ cup (40g) coarsely grated
    parmesan cheese
1¼ cups (150g) coarsely grated
    cheddar cheese
415g can pink salmon, drained,
    skin and bones removed

1 Preheat oven to 200°C/180°C fan-forced.
2 Cook pasta in large saucepan of boiling water, uncovered, until tender; drain.
3 Meanwhile, melt butter in medium saucepan. Add flour; cook, stirring, until mixture thickens and bubbles. Gradually stir in milk; stir over medium heat until sauce boils and thickens. Stir in peas, ¼ cup parmesan and ¾ cup cheddar.
4 Combine sauce mixture with pasta and salmon in shallow 2.5-litre (10-cup) oiled ovenproof dish; sprinkle with remaining combined cheeses. Bake, uncovered, in oven, about 20 minutes or until browned lightly.

preparation time **15 minutes**
cooking time **35 minutes** serves **6**
per serving 23.8g total fat (13.7g saturated fat); 2345kJ (561 cal); 51.2g carbohydrate; 33.1g protein; 3.9g fibre

cost-cutter Why would you buy pre-made gnocchi when you can make these for half the price and double the delectability? Both affordable and impressive, this recipe is perfect fare for a crowd: double the recipe and make the gnocchi to step 2. Refrigerating them overnight firms the gnocchi for even easier handling and frees up your time.

gnocchi with tomato and basil sauce

1 litre (4 cups) milk
1 cup (180g) semolina
4 egg yolks
⅔ cup (50g) finely grated parmesan cheese
2 tablespoons semolina, extra
2 tablespoons olive oil
4 cloves garlic, crushed
½ cup coarsely chopped fresh basil
2 cups (520g) bottled tomato pasta sauce
40g butter, melted
½ cup (40g) finely grated parmesan
   cheese, extra

1 Bring milk to a boil in medium saucepan. Gradually add semolina, stirring constantly. Reduce heat; simmer, stirring, about 5 minutes or until mixture thickens. Remove from heat; stir in egg yolks and cheese. Stand 5 minutes.
2 Sprinkle extra semolina on flat surface; roll semolina mixture into two x 5cm-thick sausage shapes. Wrap in plastic; refrigerate 1 hour or until firm.
3 Meanwhile, heat oil in small saucepan; cook garlic and basil, stirring, until fragrant. Add pasta sauce; bring to a boil. Reduce heat; simmer, covered, 2 minutes.
4 Preheat grill.
5 Cut refrigerated semolina into 2cm gnocchi pieces. Place gnocchi, in single layer, on oiled oven trays. Brush gnocchi with melted butter; sprinkle with extra cheese. Grill about 3 minutes or until cheese browns lightly. Serve gnocchi topped with tomato sauce and sprinkled with fresh basil leaves, if desired.

preparation time **15 minutes** cooking time **15 minutes** (plus refrigeration time) serves **6**
per serving 27.9g total fat (13.2g saturated fat); 2023kJ (484 cal); 38.7g carbohydrate; 18.4g protein; 3.2g fibre

spicy rocket pasta

Also known as capelli d'angelo, angel hair is sold as small, circular nests of a very fine, delicate pasta; its cooking time is minimal because of its extremely thin texture.

2 tablespoons olive oil
1 teaspoon dried chilli flakes
2 cloves garlic, crushed
½ teaspoon cracked black pepper
¼ cup (60ml) lemon juice
375g angel hair pasta
80g rocket
2 medium tomatoes (300g), seeded, chopped coarsely
⅔ cup firmly packed fresh basil leaves

1 Heat oil in large frying pan; cook chilli and garlic, stirring, until fragrant. Add pepper and juice; stir until hot.
2 Meanwhile, cook pasta in large saucepan of boiling water until tender; drain.
3 Combine chilli mixture and pasta in large bowl with rocket, tomato and basil.

preparation time **15 minutes**
cooking time **40 minutes** serves **4**
per serving 10.4g total fat (1.5g saturated fat); 1756kJ (420 cal); 66.4g carbohydrate; 12.1g protein; 4.8g fibre

pasta salad with green beans and tuna

375g large pasta spirals
250g green beans, trimmed, halved crossways
425g can tuna in oil
1 medium red capsicum (200g), sliced thinly
¾ cup loosely packed fresh flat-leaf parsley leaves
lemon dressing
2 cloves garlic, crushed
1 tablespoon finely grated lemon rind
1 teaspoon cracked black pepper
1 tablespoon lemon juice

1 Cook pasta in large saucepan of boiling water, uncovered, until tender; drain. Rinse pasta under cold water; drain.
2 Meanwhile, boil, steam or microwave beans until just tender; drain. Rinse under cold water; drain.
3 Drain tuna over small bowl; reserve oil for dressing. Flake tuna in large chunks with fork.
4 Make lemon dressing.
5 Place pasta, beans and tuna in large bowl with dressing and remaining ingredients; toss gently to combine.
lemon dressing Combine ingredients with reserved oil in screw-top jar; shake well.

preparation time **10 minutes**
cooking time **10 minutes** serves **4**
per serving 26g total fat (3.9g saturated fat); 2750kJ (658 cal); 67.5g carbohydrate; 35g protein; 6.2g fibre

pea and ham soup with risoni

2 teaspoons olive oil

1 medium brown onion (150g),
   chopped coarsely

2 teaspoons ground cumin

2.5 litres (10 cups) water

2 trimmed celery stalks (200g),
   chopped coarsely

2 dried bay leaves

1.5kg ham bone

1 cup (220g) risoni pasta

2 cups (240g) frozen peas

2 tablespoons finely chopped fresh mint

1 Heat oil in large saucepan; cook onion, stirring, until softened. Add cumin; cook, stirring, until fragrant. Add the water, celery, bay leaves and bone; bring to a boil. Reduce heat; simmer, covered, 1 hour, skimming occasionally.

2 Remove bone; when cool enough to handle, cut ham from bone, discarding any skin and fat. Shred ham finely.

3 Return soup to a boil; stir in ham, pasta and peas. Cook, uncovered, about 5 minutes or until pasta is tender. Sprinkle bowls of soup with mint.

preparation time **15 minutes**
cooking time **1 hour 15 minutes** serves **6**
per serving 3g total fat (0.6g saturated fat); 811kJ (194 cal); 30g carbohydrate; 9g protein; 4.6g fibre

Risoni is a small rice-shaped pasta, very similar to orzo, and is often used as the pasta of choice when making soup.

tuna spinach lasagne

20g butter
2 tablespoons plain flour
1 cup milk
¾ cup (90g) coarsely grated cheddar cheese
4 fresh lasagne sheets (200g), trimmed to
    fit baking dish
1 quantity tuna spinach mornay (see page 6)
1 cup (70g) stale breadcrumbs

1 Preheat oven to 180°C/160°C fan-forced.
2 Melt butter in small saucepan. Add flour; cook, stirring, until mixture thickens and bubbles. Gradually stir in milk; stir over medium heat until mixture boils and thickens. Stir a quarter of the cheese into white sauce.
3 Oil shallow 2-litre (8-cup) baking dish. Cover base with lasagne sheet; top with about a third of the warm mornay. Repeat layering with remaining lasagne sheets and mornay, finishing with lasagne sheet. Spread white sauce over lasagne; top with breadcrumbs and remaining cheese.
4 Bake, covered, in oven, 30 minutes; uncover, bake about 20 minutes or until browned lightly. Stand 5 minutes before serving.

preparation time **25 minutes**
cooking time **1 hour 10 minutes** serves **4**
per serving **21.7g total fat (13.4g saturated fat); 1789kJ (428 cal); 30.9g carbohydrate; 26.2g protein; 2.5g fibre**

chicken and leek lasagne

You need to purchase a large barbecued chicken weighing approximately 900g for this recipe.

60g butter
1 large leek (500g), sliced thinly
¼ cup (35g) plain flour
2 teaspoons dijon mustard
2 cups (500ml) chicken stock, warmed
3 cups (480g) shredded barbecued chicken
4 fresh lasagne sheets (200g), trimmed to
    fit baking dish
⅔ cup (80g) coarsely grated cheddar cheese

1 Preheat oven to 180°C/160°C fan-forced.
2 Melt butter in medium saucepan; cook leek, stirring, until soft. Add flour; cook, stirring, until mixture thickens and bubbles. Gradually stir in mustard and stock; stir over medium heat until mixture boils and thickens. Reserve ⅔ cup of the white sauce; stir chicken into remaining sauce.
3 Oil shallow 2-litre (8-cup) baking dish. Cover base with lasagne sheet; top with about a quarter of the warm chicken mixture. Repeat layering with remaining lasagne sheet and chicken mixture, finishing with lasagne sheet. Spread remaining quarter of the chicken mixture over lasagne; top with reserved white sauce and the cheese.
4 Bake, covered, in oven, 30 minutes; uncover, bake about 20 minutes or until browned lightly. Stand 5 minutes before serving.

preparation time **25 minutes**
cooking time **1 hour 10 minutes** serves **4**
per serving **24.8g total fat (8.5g saturated fat); 1685kJ (403 cal); 15.5g carbohydrate; 28.8g protein; 2.4g fibre**

rice

baked risotto with spicy sausage and cherry tomatoes

5 thin spicy Italian-style sausages (400g)
3½ cups (875ml) chicken stock
2 teaspoons olive oil
1 large brown onion (200g), chopped finely
1 clove garlic, crushed
1½ cups (300g) arborio rice
250g cherry tomatoes
2 tablespoons fresh marjoram leaves

1 Preheat oven to 180°C/160°C fan-forced.
2 Cook sausages, uncovered, in heated large frying pan until browned all over and cooked through. Drain on absorbent paper; slice thickly.
3 Meanwhile, bring stock to a boil in medium saucepan. Reduce heat; simmer, covered.
4 Heat oil in same frying pan; cook onion and garlic, stirring, until onion softens. Add rice; stir to coat in onion mixture. Stir in stock and sausages.
5 Place risotto mixture in large shallow ovenproof dish; cover with foil. Bake in oven 15 minutes, stirring halfway during cooking time. Uncover; bake 15 minutes. Add tomatoes; bake about 15 minutes or until tomatoes soften and rice is tender. Remove from oven, sprinkle with marjoram.

preparation time **15 minutes**
cooking time **1 hour** serves **4**
per serving 29.1g total fat (13g saturated fat); 2587kJ (619 cal); 67.1g carbohydrate; 20.1g protein; 5g fibre

chorizo fried rice

Cook 1½ cups (300g) white long-grain rice the day before making this recipe. Spread it in an even layer on a tray and refrigerate overnight. You'll also need a quarter of a small wombok.

1 teaspoon vegetable oil
2 eggs, beaten lightly
2 chorizo sausages (340g), sliced thinly
1 fresh long red chilli, sliced thinly
1 clove garlic, crushed
2cm piece fresh ginger (10g), grated
2 cups (160g) coarsely shredded wombok
1 cup (120g) frozen pea, corn and
    carrot mixture
3 cups (600g) cold cooked rice
2 tablespoons dark soy sauce

1 Heat oil in wok; cook egg over medium heat, swirling wok to form thin omelette. Remove from wok; cool. Roll omelette tightly; cut into thin strips.
2 Add chorizo to wok; stir-fry about 5 minutes or until crisp. Add chilli, garlic, ginger, wombok and frozen vegetables; stir-fry about 5 minutes or until vegetables just soften.
3 Add rice, omelette and sauce to wok; stir-fry until combined and heated through.

preparation time **15 minutes**
cooking time **20 minutes** serves **4**
per serving **28.5g total fat (9.8g saturated fat); 2278kJ (545 cal); 47.2g carbohydrate; 23.4g protein; 3.6g fibre**

vegetarian paella

2 cups (500ml) vegetable stock
3 cups (750ml) water
1 tablespoon olive oil
2 cloves garlic, crushed
1 medium red onion (170g), chopped finely
2 medium tomatoes (300g), seeded,
    chopped finely
1 medium red capsicum (200g),
    chopped finely
¼ teaspoon ground turmeric
2 teaspoons smoked sweet paprika
1¾ cups (350g) arborio rice
1 cup (120g) frozen peas
100g frozen baby beans
¼ cup (40g) sliced black olives
⅓ cup finely chopped fresh flat-leaf parsley

1 Combine stock and the water in medium saucepan; bring to a boil. Remove from heat.
2 Heat oil in large frying pan; cook garlic, onion, tomato, capsicum, turmeric and paprika, stirring, until vegetables soften. Add rice; stir to coat in spice mixture. Stir in stock mixture; bring to a boil. Reduce heat; simmer, uncovered, about 20 minutes or until rice is almost tender.
3 Sprinkle peas and beans evenly over surface of paella; simmer, covered, about 5 minutes or until rice is tender. Add olives and parsley; stand, covered, 5 minutes.

preparation time **25 minutes**
cooking time **40 minutes** serves **4**
per serving **6g total fat (1g saturated fat); 1823kJ (437 cal); 80.3g carbohydrate; 11.6g protein; 5.7g fibre**

roasted pumpkin and spinach couscous

600g piece pumpkin, chopped coarsely
1 tablespoon olive oil
1 cup (250ml) chicken stock
1 cup (250ml) water
2 cups (400g) couscous
150g trimmed spinach, shredded coarsely
½ cup (50g) roasted walnuts,
   chopped coarsely
cumin dressing
¼ cup (60ml) lemon juice
¼ cup (60ml) olive oil
1 teaspoon honey
¾ teaspoon ground cumin
½ teaspoon cayenne pepper

1 Preheat oven to 220°C/200°C fan-forced.
2 Place pumpkin, in single layer, on oven tray; drizzle with oil. Roast, uncovered, about 30 minutes or until tender, turning halfway through cooking time.
3 Meanwhile, bring stock and the water to a boil in medium saucepan. Remove from heat; stir in couscous. Cover; stand 5 minutes, fluffing with fork occasionally. Stir in spinach, cover; stand 5 minutes.
4 Make cumin dressing.
5 Combine pumpkin and couscous mixture in large bowl with nuts and dressing.
cumin dressing Combine ingredients in screw-top jar; shake well.

preparation time **15 minutes**
cooking time **30 minutes** serves **4**
per serving 28.5g total fat (3.8g saturated fat); 2930kJ (701 cal); 89g carbohydrate; 19.5g protein; 4.5g fibre

You need about 300g of spinach for this recipe, or you can use an equivalent weight of trimmed baby spinach leaves instead.

warm lentil and sausage salad

1 cup (200g) brown lentils
3 medium tomatoes (450g), quartered
1 tablespoon olive oil
1 medium brown onion (150g), chopped finely
1 teaspoon ground cumin
8 thick chicken sausages (960g)
½ cup coarsely chopped fresh flat-leaf parsley
white wine vinaigrette
⅓ cup (80ml) white wine vinegar
¼ cup (60ml) olive oil
1 clove garlic, crushed

1 Make white wine vinaigrette.

2 Preheat oven to 220°C/200°C fan-forced.

3 Cook lentils, uncovered, in large saucepan of boiling water until just tender; drain. Place lentils in large bowl with half the vinaigrette; toss gently to combine.

4 Place tomato on oven tray; drizzle with half the oil. Roast, uncovered, in oven about 10 minutes or until tender.

5 Meanwhile, heat remaining oil in large frying pan; cook onion and cumin, stirring, until onion softens. Transfer onion mixture to bowl with lentils.

6 Cook sausages in same pan until cooked through. Drain on absorbent paper.

7 Meanwhile, add remaining vinaigrette, sliced sausage, tomato and parsley to bowl with lentil mixture; toss gently to combine.

white wine vinaigrette Combine ingredients in screw-top jar; shake well.

preparation time **15 minutes**
cooking time **45 minutes** serves **4**
per serving **73.6g total fat (21g saturated fat); 4034kJ (965 cal); 28.3g carbohydrate; 41.8g protein: 16.4g fibre**

tuna and cannellini bean salad

2 cups (400g) dried cannellini beans
425g can tuna in springwater, drained
1 small red onion (100g), sliced thinly
2 trimmed celery stalks (200g), sliced thinly
italian dressing
⅓ cup (80ml) olive oil
⅓ cup (80ml) lemon juice
1 tablespoon finely chopped fresh oregano
2 cloves garlic, crushed

1 Place beans in medium bowl, cover with cold water; stand overnight, drain. Rinse under cold water; drain. Place beans in medium saucepan of boiling water; return to a boil. Reduce heat; simmer, uncovered, about 1 hour or until beans are almost tender. Drain.
2 Meanwhile, make italian dressing.
3 Combine beans and dressing in large bowl with tuna, onion and celery.
italian dressing Combine ingredients in screw-top jar; shake well.

preparation time **10 minutes (plus standing time)**
cooking time **1 hour** serves **4**
per serving 21.6g total fat (3.8g saturated fat); 1651kJ (395 cal); 17.3g carbohydrate; 28.8g protein; 8.5g fibre

lamb and burghul burgers

½ cup (80g) burghul
½ cup (125ml) boiling water
250g minced lamb
1 small brown onion (80g), chopped finely
1 small zucchini (90g), grated coarsely
¼ cup finely chopped fresh mint
1 egg
1 tablespoon olive oil
4 turkish bread rolls (660g)
½ baby cos lettuce, torn
1 large tomato (220g), sliced thinly
1 cup (240g) hummus

1 Place burghul in small bowl, cover with the boiling water; stand 10 minutes or until burghul softens and water is absorbed.
2 Combine burghul in medium bowl with lamb, onion, zucchini, mint and egg. Shape mixture into four patties.
3 Heat oil in large frying pan; cook patties, over medium heat, until browned both sides and cooked through.
4 Meanwhile, preheat grill.
5 Split rolls in half; toast cut sides. Sandwich lettuce, patties, tomato and hummus between roll halves.

preparation time **25 minutes**
cooking time **20 minutes** serves **4**
per serving 28.3g total fat (6.9g saturated fat); 3407kJ (815 cal); 94.2g carbohydrate; 38.3g protein; 14.7g fibre

cost-cutter Polenta is a cereal product deserving of more attention: why confine your choice of comfort food to just rice or pasta? Polenta isn't expensive, and a little goes a long way. Many like to eat it for breakfast, soft like porridge topped with maple syrup, or fried with bacon. It makes as good a casserole topping as béchamel or mash, and can be used in baking, from cakes to pizza bases.

chilli cheese polenta with bean and avocado salsa

1 litre (4 cups) water
1 cup (170g) polenta
¼ teaspoon chilli powder
1 cup (120g) coarsely grated cheddar cheese
1 tablespoon vegetable oil
bean and avocado salsa
3 medium tomatoes (450g), chopped coarsely
1 small red onion (100g), chopped finely
1 medium avocado (250g), chopped coarsely
420g can four-bean mix, rinsed, drained
2 tablespoons sweet chilli sauce

1 Oil 19cm-square cake pan.
2 Place the water in large saucepan; bring to a boil. Gradually stir polenta into the water; reduce heat. Simmer, stirring, about 10 minutes or until polenta thickens. Stir in chilli and cheese; spread polenta into pan, cool 10 minutes. Cover; refrigerate about 1 hour or until polenta firms.
3 Meanwhile, make bean and avocado salsa.
4 Turn polenta onto board; trim edges. Cut polenta into quarters; cut each quarter into three slices. Heat oil in large frying pan; cook polenta, uncovered, until browned both sides.
5 Serve polenta slices topped with salsa.
bean and avocado salsa Combine ingredients in medium bowl.

preparation time **10 minutes** cooking time **20 minutes (plus refrigeration time)** serves **4**
per serving **26.2g total fat (9.4g saturated fat); 2094kJ (501 cal); 44.9g carbohydrate; 17.9g protein; 8.4g fibre**

cost-cutter Making small savoury pies is a way to stretch leftover roast chicken into a second meal. Discard the chicken carcass then stir the chopped meat into a homemade white sauce with some frozen peas and carrot, a few mushrooms and a bit of chopped celery. Spoon mixture into small pie dishes, cover each with a round cut from a puff pastry sheet and bake until hot and golden on top.

lentil cottage pie

4 medium potatoes (800g), chopped coarsely
½ cup (125ml) milk, warmed
4 green onions, chopped finely
½ cup (100g) french green lentils
1 tablespoon olive oil
1 large brown onion (200g), chopped finely
1 medium red capsicum (200g), chopped coarsely
2 medium zucchini (240g), chopped coarsely
1 medium eggplant (300g), chopped coarsely
2 cloves garlic, crushed
410g can crushed tomatoes

1 Boil, steam or microwave potato until tender; drain. Mash potato in large bowl with milk and green onion until smooth.
2 Meanwhile, cook lentils in small saucepan of boiling water until just tender; drain. Rinse; drain.
3 Preheat oven to 200°C/180°C fan-forced.
4 Heat oil in medium saucepan; cook brown onion, capsicum, zucchini, eggplant and garlic, stirring, until vegetables soften. Add lentils and undrained tomato; bring to a boil. Reduce heat; simmer, about 10 minutes or until mixture has thickened.
5 Spoon mixture into lightly oiled shallow 2.5 litre (10-cup) baking dish; spread with potato. Bake, uncovered, in oven about 30 minutes or until top browns lightly.

preparation time **20 minutes**
cooking time **1 hour 15 minutes** serves **4**
per serving **7.3g total fat (1.5g saturated fat); 1384kJ (331 cal); 44.8g carbohydrate; 15.4g protein; 11.8g fibre**

italian chickpea stew

1 cup (200g) dried chickpeas
1 tablespoon olive oil
1 medium red onion (170g), chopped coarsely
2 cloves garlic, crushed
425g can chopped tomatoes
2 cups (500ml) vegetable stock
1 medium eggplant (300g), chopped coarsely
2 large zucchini (300g), chopped coarsely
2 tablespoons tomato paste
⅓ cup coarsely chopped fresh flat-leaf parsley

1 Place chickpeas in medium bowl, cover with cold water; stand overnight, drain. Rinse under cold water; drain. Place chickpeas in medium saucepan of boiling water; return to a boil. Reduce heat; simmer, uncovered, about 1 hour or until chickpeas are tender. Drain.
2 Heat oil in large saucepan; cook onion and garlic until onion softens. Add chickpeas and remaining ingredients; bring to a boil. Reduce heat; simmer, covered, 30 minutes. Uncover; simmer, about 30 minutes or until mixture thickens slightly.
3 Serve stew sprinkled with parsley, and topped with grated parmesan, if desired.

preparation time 15 minutes (plus standing time)
cooking time 2 hours 10 minutes serves 4
per serving 8.7g total fat (1.3g saturated fat); 1145kJ
(274 cal); 29g carbohydrate; 13.8g protein; 12.2g fibre

chickpea and kumara salad

1 cup (200g) dried chickpeas
1 medium red onion (170g), chopped coarsely
1 medium red capsicum (200g), sliced thickly
1 medium kumara (400g), diced into
    1cm pieces
2 cloves garlic, unpeeled
⅓ cup (80ml) olive oil
¼ cup (60ml) lemon juice
1 teaspoon english mustard
150g baby spinach leaves

1 Place chickpeas in medium bowl, cover with cold water; stand overnight, drain. Rinse under cold water; drain.
2 Preheat oven to 220°C/200°C fan-forced.
3 Place chickpeas in medium saucepan of boiling water; return to a boil. Reduce heat; simmer, uncovered, about 1 hour or until chickpeas are tender. Drain.
4 Meanwhile, toss onion, capsicum, kumara, garlic and 1 tablespoon of the oil in shallow baking dish. Bake, uncovered, in oven about 30 minutes or until kumara is tender. Cool 10 minutes; remove garlic from dish.
5 Using back of fork, crush peeled garlic in large bowl; whisk in remaining oil, juice and mustard.
6 Combine chickpeas, roasted vegetables and spinach with garlic vinaigrette in bowl.

preparation time 20 minutes (plus standing time)
cooking time 30 minutes serves 4
per serving 21.5g total fat (3g saturated fat); 1685kJ
(403 cal); 34.9g carbohydrate; 12.7g protein; 10.3g fibre

curry and lime lentil soup

2 teaspoons vegetable oil
1 tablespoon hot curry paste
1 medium brown onion (150g), chopped finely
2 cloves garlic, crushed
2cm piece fresh ginger (10g), grated
1 teaspoon cumin seeds
1 cup (200g) red lentils
2 cups (500ml) vegetable stock
2½ cups (625ml) water
400g can diced tomatoes
1 teaspoon finely grated lime rind
¼ cup (60ml) lime juice
⅓ cup finely chopped fresh flat-leaf parsley

1 Heat oil in large saucepan; cook curry paste, stirring, until fragrant. Add onion, garlic, ginger and cumin; cook, stirring, until onion softens.

2 Add lentils, stock, the water and undrained tomatoes. Bring to a boil; reduce heat. Simmer, uncovered, about 20 minutes or until lentils are softened.

3 Stir in rind and juice; return to a boil. Remove from heat; stir in parsley.

preparation time **15 minutes**
cooking time **30 minutes** serves **4**
per serving 6g **total fat (0.9g saturated fat); 991kJ (237 cal); 25.2g carbohydrate; 15.4g protein; 9.9g fibre**

cost-cutter Soups are a perfect vehicle for kitchen novices such as students or children. Choosing the vegetables, pulses and grains for homemade soup can spur both an interest in cooking and in keeping costs down. Ingredients can be added to a canned soup – fried chopped onion or bacon, fresh tomato or herbs – and served with warm bread and a salad to make a tasty, satisfying meal.

cost-cutter Chickpeas are a major source of protein in cultures either predominantly vegetarian or where meat is considered a luxury item. Used in so many of our favourite dishes (think hummus and salsa), chickpeas can be soaked, parboiled then frozen in user-friendly amounts, ready to go when your menu dictates. One cup of dried chickpeas will double in quantity after soaking.

chickpeas in spicy tomato sauce

¾ cup (150g) dried chickpeas
1 tablespoon olive oil
2 teaspoons cumin seeds
1 tablespoon ground coriander
¼ teaspoon cayenne pepper
1 medium brown onion (150g),
　chopped finely
2 cloves garlic, crushed
4cm piece fresh ginger (20g), grated
2 tablespoons tomato paste
810g can crushed tomatoes
1 cup (250ml) water
5 baby new potatoes (200g), quartered
10 baby carrots (200g), halved lengthways
½ cup coarsely chopped fresh coriander

1 Place chickpeas in medium bowl, cover with cold water; stand overnight, drain. Rinse under cold water; drain. Place chickpeas in medium saucepan of boiling water; return to a boil. Reduce heat; simmer, uncovered, about 1 hour or until tender; drain.

2 Heat oil in large saucepan; cook cumin, coriander and cayenne, stirring, until fragrant. Add onion, garlic and ginger; cook, stirring, until onion softens. Add tomato paste; cook, stirring, 2 minutes.

3 Add undrained tomatoes, the water, potato and chickpeas; bring to a boil. Reduce heat; simmer, covered, about 30 minutes, stirring occasionally, until potato is tender and mixture thickened.

4 Add carrot; cook, uncovered, about 5 minutes or until carrot is tender. Remove from heat; stir in coriander.

preparation time 20 minutes (plus standing time)
cooking time 1 hour 40 minutes serves 4
per serving 7.4g total fat (1g saturated fat); 1062kJ
(254 cal); 31.1g carbohydrate; 7.4g protein; 10.6g fibre

potato, garlic and oregano pizza

2 teaspoons dry yeast
½ teaspoon caster sugar
¾ cup (180ml) warm water
2 cups (300g) plain flour
1 teaspoon salt
2 tablespoons olive oil
2 tablespoons polenta
⅓ cup loosely packed fresh oregano leaves
6 small potatoes (720g), sliced thinly
3 cloves garlic, crushed
2 tablespoons olive oil, extra
½ teaspoon sea salt flakes
1 tablespoon fresh oregano leaves, extra

1 Combine yeast, sugar and the water in small bowl, cover; stand in warm place about 10 minutes or until mixture is frothy.
2 Sift flour and salt into large bowl; stir in yeast mixture and oil. Mix to a soft dough. Bring dough together with hands, adding extra water if necessary.
3 Knead dough on floured surface about 10 minutes or until smooth and elastic. Place in oiled bowl, cover; stand in warm place about 1 hour or until doubled in size.
4 Preheat oven to 240°C/220°C fan-forced. Lightly oil two oven trays.
5 Punch dough down with fist; knead on floured surface until smooth. Divide dough in half; roll halves to 20cm x 30cm rectangle; place on trays. Sprinkle dough with polenta; prick with fork.
6 Divide oregano leaves between bases then layer with potato, overlapping slightly. Brush combined garlic and extra oil over potato.
7 Bake about 20 minutes or until potato is tender and bases are crisp. Sprinkle pizzas with sea salt and extra oregano before serving.

preparation time **25 minutes (plus standing time)**
cooking time **20 minutes serves 4**
per serving **19.5g total fat (2.8g saturated fat); 2328kJ (557 cal); 79.1g carbohydrate; 12.8g protein; 6.1g fibre**

free-form caramelised leek tart

2 tablespoons olive oil
2 medium brown onions (300g), sliced thinly
2 medium leeks (700g), trimmed, sliced thinly
1 tablespoon fresh thyme leaves
2 cups (400g) ricotta cheese
⅓ cup (25g) coarsely grated parmesan cheese
1 egg, separated
4 sheets ready-rolled shortcrust pastry

1 Heat oil in large frying pan; cook onion and leek, stirring, about 15 minutes or until mixture starts to caramelise. Stir in thyme; cool.
2 Meanwhile, combine ricotta, parmesan and egg yolk in small bowl.
3 Preheat oven to 200°C/180°C fan-forced. Oil two oven trays; line with baking paper.
4 Using 20cm plate as a guide, cut 1 round from each pastry sheet; place two rounds on each tray. Divide ricotta mixture among rounds, leaving 4cm border around edges.
5 Divide leek mixture over rounds. Turn border of each tart up around filling; brush upturned edges with egg white. Bake about 35 minutes or until pastry is browned lightly.

preparation time **30 minutes**
cooking time **50 minutes** serves **4**
per serving 70g total fat (34.3g saturated fat); 4531kJ (1084 cal); 83.2g carbohydrate; 28.3g protein; 7.1g fibre

cost-cutter Buy twice the amount of ricotta called for here and bake the extra 400g pressed into a 20cm-round greased cake pan in a moderately slow oven for about 15 minutes or until ricotta firms slightly. Baked ricotta can be used crumbled into salads, pasta, frittatas or pizza toppings, and it's delicious (and lighter than butter) for breakfast spread over toasted turkish bread.

vegetable soup

*You need approximately 1kg silver beet
for this recipe.*

1 tablespoon vegetable oil
2 large brown onions (400g), chopped finely
2 large carrots (360g), chopped coarsely
8 trimmed celery stalks (800g),
    chopped coarsely
3 cloves garlic, crushed
1 litre (4 cups) vegetable stock
1 litre (4 cups) water
¾ cup (165g) soup pasta
2 medium zucchini (240g), sliced thickly
250g trimmed silver beet, chopped coarsely

1 Heat oil in large saucepan; cook onion,
carrot, celery and garlic, stirring, until
vegetables soften.
2 Add stock and the water; bring to a boil.
Reduce heat; simmer, uncovered, 10 minutes.
Add pasta and zucchini; simmer, uncovered,
stirring occasionally, about 5 minutes or until
pasta is tender. Add silver beet; cook, stirring,
until silver beet just wilts.

preparation time **15 minutes**
cooking time **35 minutes** serves **4**
per serving **6.8g total fat (1.2g saturated fat); 1296kJ (310
cal); 43.5g carbohydrate; 12.4g protein; 11.5g fibre**

spinach and corn pasties

1 tablespoon vegetable oil
2 medium potatoes (400g), diced into
    1cm pieces
1 small brown onion (80g), chopped finely
250g frozen spinach, thawed, drained
2 x 310g cans creamed corn
3 sheets ready-rolled shortcrust pastry
2 tablespoons milk

1 Heat half the oil in large frying pan; cook
potato, stirring, until browned lightly. Add
onion; cook, stirring, until soft. Combine
potato, onion, spinach and corn in large bowl.
2 Preheat oven to 200°C/180°C fan-forced.
Oil two oven trays.
3 Cut pastry sheets in half diagonally. Divide
filling among triangles, placing on one side;
fold pastry in half to enclose filling, pressing
edges with fork to seal.
4 Place pasties on trays; brush with milk. Bake
about 30 minutes or until browned lightly.
Serve with sweet chilli sauce, if desired.

preparation time **20 minutes**
cooking time **45 minutes** serves **6**
per serving **27.1g total fat (12.6g saturated fat); 2291kJ
(548 cal); 62.7g carbohydrate; 9.8g protein; 7.5g fibre**

cost-cutter Fry another two sliced eggplants, as described below, to the end of step 3. Alternate the slices, in a shallow medium baking dish, by layering with fried garlic and onion, tomato passata, sliced mozzarella and a sprinkle of fresh oregano. Bake, uncovered, in a moderate oven until mixture firms. Cool, cover and refrigerate for a day or two after you eat the burgers; reheat and serve with penne.

chilli and mint eggplant burgers

¼ cup (35g) plain flour
2 eggs
½ cup (85g) polenta
1 teaspoon hot paprika
1 medium eggplant (300g)
vegetable oil, for shallow-frying
1 large loaf turkish bread (430g), quartered
8 large butter lettuce leaves
80g cheddar cheese, cut into 4 slices
½ cup loosely packed fresh mint leaves
⅓ cup (80ml) sweet chilli sauce

1 Place flour in small shallow bowl; beat eggs in second small shallow bowl; combine polenta and paprika in third small shallow bowl.

2 Slice eggplant into 8 slices crossways; discard two skin-side pieces. Coat slices, one at a time, in flour, shake away excess, dip in egg then coat in polenta mixture.

3 Heat oil in large frying pan; shallow-fry eggplant, in batches, until browned lightly both sides. Drain on absorbent paper.

4 Meanwhile, preheat grill.

5 Halve each quarter of bread horizontally. Toast cut sides under grill.

6 Sandwich lettuce, eggplant, cheese, mint and sauce between toasted bread quarters.

preparation time **20 minutes**
cooking time **10 minutes** serves **4**
per serving 23g total fat (6g saturated fat); 2684kJ (642 cal); 77.9g carbohydrate; 24.3g protein; 12.3g fibre

spanish cheese and tomato tortilla

4 green onions, sliced thickly
1 medium red capsicum (200g),
    chopped coarsely
2 cloves garlic, crushed
1 fresh long red chilli, chopped finely
2 medium tomatoes (300g), chopped coarsely
200g fetta cheese, crumbled
8 eggs
300ml cream
¼ cup firmly packed fresh flat-leaf
    parsley leaves, chopped coarsely

1 Heat oiled 26cm frying pan; cook onion, capsicum, garlic and chilli, stirring, until vegetables are just tender. Remove from heat; stir in tomato and cheese.
2 Whisk eggs, cream and parsley in large jug. Pour over capsicum mixture; stir gently.
3 Preheat grill.
4 Return pan to low heat; cook tortilla, uncovered, until just set. Place pan under grill to brown tortilla top (protect handle with foil). Cut into wedges to serve.

preparation time **15 minutes**
cooking time **20 minutes** serves **4**
per serving **49.9g total fat (29g saturated fat); 2424kJ (580 cal); 7.6g carbohydrate; 25.6g protein; 2.2g fibre**

cauliflower salad with lemon mayonnaise

200g button mushrooms, halved
1 clove garlic, crushed
2 tablespoons olive oil
1 tablespoon finely grated lemon rind
¼ cup (60ml) lemon juice
1 small cauliflower (1kg), trimmed,
    cut into florets
1 cup (300g) mayonnaise
1 teaspoon water
1 medium red onion (170g), sliced thinly
150g baby spinach leaves

1 Combine mushrooms, garlic, oil, half the rind and two-thirds of the juice in small bowl, cover; refrigerate 1 hour.
2 Meanwhile, boil, steam or microwave cauliflower until just tender; drain. Rinse under cold water; drain.
3 Combine remaining rind, remaining juice, mayonnaise and the water in small bowl.
4 Just before serving, combine mushrooms, cauliflower, onion and spinach in large bowl; drizzle with lemon mayonnaise.

preparation time **15 minutes (plus refrigeration time)**
cooking time **10 minutes** serves **4**
per serving **34.1g total fat (4g saturated fat); 1856kJ (444 cal); 22.8g carbohydrate; 9g protein; 7.4g fibre**

chicken and vegetable pasties

2 teaspoons vegetable oil
2 cloves garlic, crushed
1 medium brown onion (150g),
    chopped finely
1½ cups (240g) coarsely chopped
    leftover cooked chicken
2 cups (240g) frozen pea, corn and
    carrot mixture
2 teaspoons dijon mustard
½ cup (120g) sour cream
¼ cup (30g) coarsely grated cheddar cheese
4 sheets ready-rolled puff pastry
1 egg, beaten lightly

1 Preheat oven to 220°C/200°C fan-forced.
Lightly oil oven tray.
2 Heat oil in large frying pan; cook garlic
and onion, stirring, until onion softens.
3 Add chicken, frozen vegetables, mustard,
sour cream and cheese; stir until hot.
4 Cut one 22cm round from each pastry
sheet. Place a quarter of the filling in centre
of each round. Brush edge of pastry with egg;
fold over to enclose filling, pinching edge
together to seal.
5 Place pasties on tray; brush with remaining
egg. Bake in oven about 30 minutes or until
browned lightly.

preparation time **15 minutes**
cooking time **30 minutes** serves **4**
per serving **62.5g total fat (32.3g saturated fat); 4063kJ
(972 cal); 69.1g carbohydrate; 31.4g protein; 5.9g fibre**

smashed roast potato and thyme gratin

50g butter
1 medium brown onion (150g), sliced thinly
600g roast potatoes, halved
2 tablespoons plain flour
1 cup (250ml) milk
2 teaspoons finely chopped fresh thyme
1 cup (120g) coarsely grated cheddar cheese

1 Preheat oven to 220°C/200°C fan-forced. Oil four 1-cup (250ml) shallow ovenproof baking dishes.

2 Melt 10g of the butter in medium saucepan; cook onion, stirring, until softened.

3 Meanwhile, use potato masher to gently crush potato in large bowl; stir in onion mixture.

4 Melt remaining butter in same pan, add flour; cook, stirring, until mixture thickens and bubbles. Gradually stir in milk; cook, stirring, until white sauce boils and thickens. Remove from heat; stir in thyme and half the cheese.

5 Stir white sauce into potato mixture. Spoon gratin mixture into dishes; sprinkle each with remaining cheese. Bake in oven about 20 minutes or until browned lightly.

preparation time **15 minutes**
cooking time **30 minutes** serves **4 as a side dish**
per serving **29.1g total fat (16.5g saturated fat); 2128kJ (509 cal); 42.8g carbohydrate; 17.1g protein; 4.8g fibre**

pork salad with chilli plum dressing

1 medium wombok (1kg), shredded finely
½ cup finely shredded fresh mint
1 small red onion (100g), sliced thinly
400g leftover roast pork, shredded finely
½ cup firmly packed fresh mint leaves
chilli plum dressing
½ cup (150g) mayonnaise
½ cup (125ml) plum sauce
1 teaspoon dried chilli flakes
2 tablespoons water

1 Make chilli plum dressing.
2 Combine half the dressing in large bowl with wombok, shredded mint, onion and half the pork.
3 Divide wombok mixture among serving plates; top with remaining pork and mint leaves, drizzle with remaining dressing.
chilli plum dressing Whisk ingredients in small bowl.

preparation time **20 minutes** serves **4**
per serving 16.6g total fat (4g saturated fat); 1889kJ (452 cal); 31.7g carbohydrate; 32.8g protein; 8.9g fibre

lamb fritters with spicy yogurt

2 teaspoons ground cumin
1 cup (280g) Greek-style yogurt
1 egg
1¾ cups (260g) self-raising flour
1½ cups (375ml) buttermilk
150g piece pumpkin, grated finely
2 green onions, chopped finely
300g leftover roast lamb, chopped coarsely
vegetable oil, for shallow-frying

1 Dry-fry cumin in large frying pan, stirring, until fragrant.
2 Combine yogurt with half the cumin in small bowl.
3 Combine egg, flour and buttermilk in large bowl with pumpkin, onion, lamb and remaining cumin; mix well.
4 Heat oil in same pan; shallow-fry quarter cups of batter, in batches, until fritters are browned lightly. Drain on absorbent paper; serve with yogurt.

preparation time **10 minutes**
cooking time **20 minutes** serves **4**
per serving 49.2g total fat (13.3g saturated fat); 3511kJ (840 cal); 60.3g carbohydrate; 37.6g protein; 3g fibre

We used leftover roasted kumara, potato, red onion, zucchini and capsicum in this recipe, but any remaining roasted vegetables are suitable to use.

chorizo and roast vegetable frittata

6 eggs
½ cup (125ml) cream
⅓ cup (40g) coarsely grated cheddar cheese
1 chorizo sausage (170g), sliced thinly
1½ cups coarsely chopped leftover
    roasted vegetables
¼ teaspoon cayenne pepper

1 Preheat oven to 180°C/160°C fan-forced. Oil 19cm-square cake pan; line base with baking paper, extending paper slightly above edges.
2 Whisk eggs, cream and cheese together in large jug.
3 Cook chorizo in medium frying pan, stirring, until browned and crisp. Drain on absorbent paper.
4 Place vegetables in pan; top with chorizo. Pour egg mixture over chorizo; sprinkle with cayenne.
5 Bake in oven about 30 minutes or until frittata is set; stand 10 minutes before cutting.

preparation time **10 minutes (plus standing time)**
cooking time **35 minutes** serves **4**
per serving **37g total fat (17.1g saturated fat); 1902kJ (455 cal); 7.2g carbohydrate; 23.4g protein; 2.3g fibre**

antipasto picnic loaf

2 medium red capsicums (400g)
1 medium eggplant (300g), sliced thinly
2 large flat mushrooms (160g), sliced thinly
1 round cob loaf (450g)
⅓ cup (95g) wholegrain mustard
⅓ cup (100g) mayonnaise
200g leftover roast beef, sliced thinly
½ small green coral lettuce, trimmed,
   leaves separated

1 Preheat oven to 220°C/200°C fan-forced.
2 Quarter capsicums; discard seeds and membranes. Roast, skin-side up, until skin blisters and blackens. Cover capsicum pieces with plastic or paper for 5 minutes; peel away skin.
3 Place eggplant and mushrooms on lightly oiled oven tray. Roast about 15 minutes or until tender; cool.
4 Cut shallow lid from top of loaf; remove soft bread inside, leaving 2cm-thick shell.
5 Spread half the combined mustard and mayonnaise inside bread shell and lid. Place beef inside bread shell; top with mushroom then capsicum and eggplant, pressing layers down firmly. Spread with remaining mayonnaise mixture; top with lettuce. Replace lid; press down firmly.
6 Wrap loaf tightly with kitchen string and plastic wrap; refrigerate 2 hours or until required.

preparation time 20 minutes (plus refrigeration time)
cooking time 25 minutes serves 4
per serving 24g total fat (3.6g saturated fat); 2692kJ (644 cal); 67.7g carbohydrate; 34.5g protein; 8.9g fibre

You need to cook 2 cups (400g) of white long-grain rice the day before making this recipe. Spread evenly onto a tray; refrigerate overnight.

chicken fried rice

1 tablespoon vegetable oil
2 eggs, beaten lightly
3 rindless bacon rashers (195g),
    chopped coarsely
2 cloves garlic, crushed
2cm piece fresh ginger (10g), grated
1½ cups (240g) coarsely chopped leftover
    cooked chicken
4 cups cold cooked rice
1 cup (140g) frozen pea and corn mixture
¼ cup (60ml) light soy sauce
1 cup (80g) bean sprouts
6 green onions, sliced thinly

1 Heat half the oil in wok; cook egg over medium heat, swirling wok to form thin omelette. Remove from wok; cool. Roll omelette tightly; cut into thin strips.
2 Heat remaining oil in wok; stir-fry bacon, garlic and ginger until bacon is crisp.
3 Add chicken; stir-fry 1 minute. Add rice, frozen vegetables and sauce; stir-fry until hot. Add sprouts, onion and omelette; stir-fry 1 minute.

preparation time **10 minutes**
cooking time **15 minutes** serves **4**
per serving **21.9g** total fat (5.9g saturated fat); 2362kJ (565 cal); 52.6g carbohydrate; 37.2g protein; 3.8g fibre

beef, garlic and silver beet pasta bake

250g small macaroni
2 teaspoons vegetable oil
4 cloves garlic, crushed
250g trimmed silver beet, finely shredded
300g sour cream
5 cups bolognese sauce (see page 31)
½ cup (60g) coarsely grated cheddar cheese

1 Preheat oven to 200°C/180°C fan-forced.
2 Cook pasta in large saucepan of boiling
water, uncovered, until just tender; drain.
Rinse under cold water; drain.
3 Meanwhile, heat oil in large frying pan;
cook garlic, stirring, 1 minute. Add silver beet;
cook, stirring, until wilted. Stir in pasta and
sour cream.
4 Spread half the bolognese into shallow
3-litre (12-cup) baking dish. Layer with half
the silver beet mixture; top with remaining
bolognese then remaining silver beet mixture.
Sprinkle cheese over mixture.
5 Bake, uncovered, in oven about 20 minutes
or until browned and heated through.

preparation time 10 minutes
cooking time 40 minutes serves 6
per serving 38.2g total fat (20.5g saturated fat); 2654kJ
(635 cal); 38.7g carbohydrate; 31.7g protein; 6g fibre

curried beef and lentils

½ cup (100g) yellow split peas
2 teaspoons vegetable oil
1 small brown onion (80g), sliced thinly
1 large tomato (220g), chopped coarsely
1 tablespoon curry powder
5 cups bolognese sauce (see page 31)
⅓ cup (55g) raisins
1 loaf turkish bread (430g), quartered
¾ cup (200g) Greek-style yogurt

1 Cook split peas in medium saucepan
of boiling water, uncovered, until just
tender; drain.
2 Meanwhile, heat oil in medium frying
pan; cook onion, tomato and curry powder,
stirring, until onion softens. Add split peas,
bolognese and raisins; bring to a boil.
3 Meanwhile, preheat grill.
4 Halve bread quarters crossways; toast
cut sides under grill.
5 Serve curried beef with toast; top with
yogurt. Sprinkle with fresh coriander,
if desired.

preparation time 10 minutes
cooking time 30 minutes serves 4
per serving 29.5g total fat (10.7g saturated fat); 3603kJ
(862 cal); 88.9g carbohydrate; 53.3g protein; 12.1g fibre

desserts

french apple tart

50g butter
⅓ cup (75g) firmly packed brown sugar
¼ cup (60ml) cream
¼ teaspoon ground cinnamon
3 medium apples (450g), peeled, cored,
  sliced thickly
1 sheet ready-rolled puff pastry

1 Preheat oven to 240°C/220°C fan-forced.
2 Stir butter, sugar, cream and cinnamon in medium saucepan over low heat until sugar dissolves; bring to a boil. Add apple, reduce heat; simmer, uncovered, without stirring, about 5 minutes or until apple is tender.
3 Spread apple mixture into 23cm pie dish.
4 Cut 24cm round from pastry sheet; place round on top of apple mixture. Bake in oven about 20 minutes or until pastry is browned lightly. Stand 5 minutes; turn tart, apple-side up, onto serving plate.

preparation time **10 minutes**
cooking time **30 minutes** serves **6**
per serving **16.9g total fat (10.3g saturated fat); 1175kJ (281 cal); 29.7g carbohydrate; 2g protein; 1.5g fibre**

cost-cutter Some of the world's great recipes are based on using yesterday's stale bread rather than wasting it: just think about panzanella, fattoush, french toast and half a dozen wintry Italian soups. Bread and butter pudding is another classic example. And we're not just talking plain white bread alone here: brioche, panettone, challah and croissant all make a mean bread pudding.

banana caramel bread and butter pudding

2 cups (500ml) cream
1½ cups (375ml) milk
⅓ cup (75g) caster sugar
1 teaspoon vanilla extract
4 eggs
½ cup (200g) caramel Top 'n' Fill
¼ cup (60ml) cream, extra
2 large overripe bananas (460g), sliced thickly
1 small french bread stick (120g), sliced thickly

1 Preheat oven to 180°C/160°C fan-forced. Grease shallow 2-litre (8-cup) ovenproof dish.
2 Heat cream, milk, sugar and extract in medium saucepan. Whisk eggs in large bowl; gradually whisk in hot cream mixture.
3 Combine caramel mixture and extra cream in small saucepan; cook, stirring over low heat, until smooth.
4 Place banana, in single layer, into dish. Layer bread on top of banana, overlapping slices slightly; drizzle with caramel cream then pour hot cream mixture over bread, taking care not to dislodge slices.
5 Place dish in larger baking dish; add enough boiling water to come halfway up sides of dish. Bake in oven about 1 hour 20 minutes or until pudding sets. Remove pudding from water; stand 5 minutes before serving.

preparation time 10 minutes
cooking time 1 hour 30 minutes serves 6
per serving 45.6g total fat (28.5g saturated fat); 3143kJ (752 cal); 42.4g carbohydrate; 15.3g protein; 1.9g fibre

apple and blackberry jellies

85g packet blackcurrant jelly crystals
1 cup (150g) frozen blackberries
1 medium apple (150g), peeled, cored,
   chopped finely
½ cup (125ml) thickened cream
1 tablespoon icing sugar

1 Prepare jelly according to packet instructions.
2 Divide blackberries and apple among
four ¾-cup (180ml) glasses then pour jelly
over the top. Refrigerate about 3 hours or
until jelly has set.
3 Beat cream and icing sugar in small bowl
with electric mixer until soft peaks form.
Serve jellies topped with whipped cream.

preparation time 10 minutes (plus refrigeration time)
serves 4
per serving 11.6g total fat (7.6g saturated fat); 986kJ
(239 cal); 30.1g carbohydrate; 2.9g protein; 1.4g fibre

white chocolate and
black cherry creamed rice

1.5 litres (6 cups) milk
⅔ cup (130g) arborio rice
2 tablespoons caster sugar
90g white chocolate, chopped finely
425g can seedless black cherries, drained

1 Combine milk, rice, sugar and half the
chocolate in medium saucepan; bring to
a boil. Reduce heat; simmer over very low
heat, stirring often, about 40 minutes or
until rice is tender.
2 Serve rice warm, topped with cherries
and remaining chocolate. Serve sprinkled
with nutmeg, if desired.

preparation time 5 minutes
cooking time 50 minutes serves 6
per serving 22.3g total fat (14.4g saturated fat); 2261kJ
(541 cal); 67.9g carbohydrate; 22.3g protein; 1.1g fibre

We used arborio rice in this recipe
but you could use calrose, a white
medium-grain rice, instead.

You need approximately half a large seedless watermelon (about 3kg in weight) for this recipe. You can juice the other half with an orange or two, or simply slice it thickly and include it in a packed lunch.

watermelon and mint granita

2 cups (500ml) water
1 cup (220g) white sugar
1.6kg coarsely chopped watermelon
2 cups firmly packed fresh mint leaves

1 Combine the water and sugar in medium saucepan. Stir over low heat, without boiling, until sugar dissolves; bring to a boil. Reduce heat; simmer, uncovered, without stirring, about 5 minutes or until syrup thickens slightly but does not colour.

2 Blend or process watermelon and mint, in batches, until almost smooth; push batches through sieve into large bowl. Add sugar syrup; stir to combine.

3 Pour mixture into two 20cm x 30cm lamington pans, cover with foil; freeze about 3 hours or until almost set.

4 Using fork, scrape granita from bottom and sides of pans, mixing frozen with unfrozen mixture. Cover, return to freezer. Repeat process every hour for about 4 hours or until large ice crystals form and granita has a dry, shard-like appearance. Scrape again with fork before serving.

preparation time **10 minutes (plus freezing time)** cooking time **10 minutes** serves **8** per serving **0.5g total fat (0g saturated fat); 698kJ (167 cal); 38.1g carbohydrate; 1g protein; 2.1g fibre**

Streusel can be frozen for up to one week. The fruit mixture can be cooked and stored, covered, in the refrigerator overnight.

apple and marmalade streusel puddings

20g butter
4 medium apples (600g), peeled, cored, sliced thinly
2 tablespoons water
1 tablespoon caster sugar
½ cup (170g) orange marmalade

streusel
½ cup (75g) plain flour
¼ cup (35g) self-raising flour
⅓ cup (75g) firmly packed brown sugar
½ teaspoon ground cinnamon
100g butter, chopped

1 Make streusel.
2 Preheat oven to 200°C/180°C fan-forced.
3 Melt butter in medium frying pan; cook apple, the water and sugar, stirring, about 10 minutes or until apple is tender. Stir in marmalade.
4 Grease four ¾-cup (180ml) ovenproof dishes; divide apple mixture among dishes.
5 Coarsely grate streusel onto baking paper; sprinkle over apple mixture. Bake in oven about 20 minutes or until browned lightly.
streusel Blend or process all ingredients until combined. Roll into a ball; wrap in plastic. Freeze streusel about 1 hour or until firm.

preparation time **15 minutes (plus freezing time)**
cooking time **30 minutes** serves 4
per serving 25.1g total fat (16.3g saturated fat); 2458kJ (588 cal); 8.2g carbohydrate; 3.4g protein; 3.6g fibre

berry trifle

1 tablespoon custard powder
2 teaspoons white sugar
1 cup milk
300ml thickened cream
2 teaspoons icing sugar
1 teaspoon vanilla extract
12 sponge-finger biscuits (180g)
1 cup (250ml) apple juice
300g frozen mixed berries

1 Combine custard powder with white sugar and milk in small saucepan; stir over low heat until custard boils and thickens.
2 Beat cream, icing sugar and extract in small bowl with electric mixer until soft peaks form.
3 Dip biscuits, one at a time, in juice; cover base of 1.5-litre (6-cup) serving dish with some of the biscuits. Top with custard and half the berries. Top with remaining dipped biscuits, cream and berries. Refrigerate 2 hours.

preparation time 20 minutes (plus refrigeration time)
cooking time 10 minutes serves 6
per serving 21.4g total fat (13.6g saturated fat); 1434kJ (343 cal); 31.4g carbohydrate; 5.7g protein; 1.5g fibre

individual tiramisu

1 teaspoon white sugar
2 teaspoons instant coffee granules
1 teaspoon cocoa powder, sifted
⅔ cup (160ml) boiling water
250g cream cheese, softened
300ml cream
¾ cup (120g) icing sugar
6 sponge-finger biscuits (90g)
2 teaspoons cocoa powder, extra

1 Blend white sugar, coffee and cocoa with the water in small bowl; cool.
2 Beat cheese in small bowl with electric mixer until smooth. Add cream and icing sugar; beat until smooth.
3 Halve biscuits crossways; dip in coffee mixture. Divide half the biscuits among four 1¼-cup (310ml) glasses. Divide half the cream mixture among glasses; top with remaining biscuits then remaining cream mixture. Refrigerate 30 minutes. Serve dusted with sifted extra cocoa powder.

preparation time 20 minutes (plus refrigeration time)
serves 4
per serving 49.5g total fat (31.8g saturated fat); 2805kJ (671 cal); 48.3g carbohydrate; 9g protein; 0.4g fibre

cost-cutter Traditional pavlovas will only call for egg whites, *a lot* of egg whites. It's criminal to waste the yolks, especially when you can freeze them for another day: drop a single yolk into each section of an ice block tray; cover the tray and freeze, popping out yolks as your needs dictate. Some recipes that call for lots of egg yolks are hollandaise, aïoli, pots de crème and zabaglione.

warm chocolate pavlovas

2 egg whites
1⅓ cups (215g) icing sugar
⅓ cup (80ml) boiling water
1 tablespoon cocoa powder, sifted
500ml chocolate ice-cream
chocolate custard sauce
1 tablespoon cornflour
1 tablespoon cocoa powder, sifted
1 tablespoon caster sugar
1 cup (125ml) milk
2 egg yolks

1 Preheat oven to 180°C/160°C fan-forced. Line large oven tray with baking paper.
2 Beat egg whites, icing sugar and the water in small bowl with electric mixer about 10 minutes or until firm peaks form.
3 Fold sifted cocoa into meringue. Drop six equal amounts of mixture onto tray; use the back of a spoon to create well in centre of mounds. Bake about 25 minutes or until firm to touch.
4 Meanwhile, make chocolate custard sauce.
5 Serve pavlovas straight from the oven, topped with ice-cream and sauce.
chocolate custard sauce Blend cornflour, cocoa and sugar with milk in small saucepan. Stir in egg yolks. Stir over heat until sauce boils and thickens.

preparation time **5 minutes**
cooking time **35 minutes** serves **4**
per serving **14.5g total fat (9g saturated fat); 2011kJ (481 cal); 79.5g carbohydrate; 7.4g protein; 0.2g fibre**

cakes

semolina and yogurt lemon-syrup cake

250g butter
1 tablespoon finely grated lemon rind
1 cup (220g) caster sugar
3 eggs, separated
1 cup (150g) self-raising flour
1 cup (160g) semolina
1 cup (280g) yogurt
lemon syrup
1 cup (220g) caster sugar
⅓ cup (80ml) lemon juice

1 Preheat oven to 180°C/160°C fan-forced. Grease and flour 20cm baba pan (or deep 19cm-round cake pan), shaking away any excess flour.
2 Beat butter, rind and sugar in small bowl with electric mixer until light and fluffy. Beat in egg yolks. Transfer mixture to large bowl; stir in flour, semolina and yogurt.
3 Beat egg whites in small bowl with electric mixer until soft peaks form; fold egg whites, into cake mixture, in two batches. Spread mixture into pan; bake about 50 minutes.
4 Meanwhile, combine ingredients for lemon syrup in small saucepan; stir over heat until sugar dissolves. Bring to a boil without stirring; remove from heat.
5 Stand cake 5 minutes; turn onto wire rack set over tray. Pierce cake all over with skewer; pour hot lemon syrup over hot cake.

preparation time **15 minutes**
cooking time **50 minutes** serves **8**
per serving **29.1g total fat (1.5g saturated fat); 2650kJ (634 cal); 83.8g carbohydrate; 8.5g protein; 1.4g fibre**

honey spice sponge cake

2 eggs
½ cup (110g) caster sugar
⅓ cup (50g) wheaten cornflour
1½ tablespoons custard powder
1 teaspoon mixed spice
½ teaspoon cream of tartar
¼ teaspoon bicarbonate of soda
300ml thickened cream
2 tablespoons honey
1 tablespoon icing sugar

1 Preheat oven to 180°C/160°C fan-forced. Grease 25cm x 30cm swiss roll pan; line base with baking paper, extending paper 5cm over long sides.

2 Beat eggs and ⅓ cup of the sugar in small bowl with electric mixer about 10 minutes or until thick and creamy.

3 Meanwhile, triple-sift cornflour, custard powder, spice, cream of tartar and soda onto baking paper. Sift flour mixture over egg mixture; fold ingredients together. Spread mixture into pan; bake 10 minutes.

4 Place a piece of baking paper cut the same size as pan on bench; sprinkle evenly with remaining sugar. Turn cake onto sugared paper; peel lining paper away. Cool.

5 Beat cream and honey in small bowl with electric mixer until firm peaks form.

6 Cut edges from all sides of sponge then cut widthways into three rectangles. Place one piece of sponge on plate; spread with half the cream mixture. Top with second piece of sponge and remaining cream. Finish with remaining piece sponge and dust with sifted icing sugar.

preparation time **15 minutes**
cooking time **10 minutes** serves **6**
per serving **20.1g total fat (12.6g saturated fat); 1480kJ (354 cal); 39.9g carbohydrate; 3.7g protein; 0.1g fibre**

chocolate coconut cakes

⅔ cup (150g) firmly packed brown sugar
¼ cup (25g) cocoa powder
½ cup (75g) self-raising flour
½ cup (75g) plain flour
⅓ cup (25g) desiccated coconut
125g butter, melted
1 egg
⅓ cup (80ml) milk
chocolate butter cream
70g butter, softened
1 tablespoon milk
¾ cup (120g) icing sugar
2 tablespoons cocoa powder, sifted

1 Preheat oven to 160°C/140°C fan-forced.
Grease 6-hole texas (¾-cup/180ml) muffin pan.
2 Sift sugar, cocoa and flours in medium bowl;
stir in coconut, butter and combined egg and
milk. Divide mixture among pan holes; bake
about 35 minutes. Stand 5 minutes; turn onto
wire rack to cool.
3 Make chocolate butter cream; spread over
cold cakes.
chocolate butter cream Beat ingredients in small
bowl with electric mixer until light and fluffy.

preparation time **25 minutes**
cooking time **30 minutes** makes **6**
per cake **32.1g** total fat (**18.9g** saturated fat); **2404kJ**
(**575 cal**); **64.8g** carbohydrate; **6.1g** protein; **1.9g** fibre

pineapple sultana loaf

440g can crushed pineapple in juice, drained
1 cup (150g) self-raising flour
½ cup (110g) caster sugar
1 cup (80g) desiccated coconut
1 cup (160g) sultanas
1 egg, beaten lightly
½ cup (125ml) milk

1 Preheat oven to 180°C/160°C fan-forced.
Grease 14cm x 21cm loaf pan; line base with
baking paper, extending paper 5cm above
long sides of pan.
2 Combine ingredients in large bowl. Pour
mixture into pan; bake about 50 minutes.
Stand loaf in pan 10 minutes; turn, top-side
up, onto wire rack to cool.

preparation time **15 minutes**
cooking time **55 minutes** serves **8**
per serving **8.1g** total fat (**6.4g** saturated fat); **1225kJ**
(**293 cal**); **48.2g** carbohydrate; **4.6g** protein; **3.7g** fibre

cost-cutter You need 2 large overripe bananas (460g) for this recipe. Never throw away bruised or blackened bananas: just pop them in the freezer as they are, to have on hand whenever you want to make this recipe again. Overripe frozen bananas can also be thawed and mashed for use in making banana bread, pancakes, breakfast smoothies or spread with peanut butter for a yummy sandwich.

banana and cinnamon muffins

2 cups (300g) self-raising flour
⅓ cup (50g) plain flour
1 teaspoon ground cinnamon
½ teaspoon bicarbonate of soda
½ cup (110g) firmly packed brown sugar
1 cup mashed banana
2 eggs
¾ cup (180ml) buttermilk
⅓ cup (80ml) vegetable oil
½ teaspoon ground cinnamon, extra
cream cheese topping
125g cream cheese, softened
¼ cup (40g) icing sugar

1 Preheat oven to 200°C/180°C fan-forced. Grease 12-hole (⅓-cup/80ml) muffin pan.
2 Sift flours, cinnamon, soda and sugar into large bowl; stir in banana then combined eggs, buttermilk and oil.
3 Divide mixture among pan holes; bake muffins about 20 minutes. Stand muffins in pan 5 minutes; turn onto wire rack to cool.
4 Make cream cheese topping. Spread cold muffins with topping; sprinkle with extra cinnamon.
cream cheese topping Beat ingredients in small bowl with electric mixer until smooth.

preparation time **20 minutes**
cooking time **20 minutes** makes **12**
per muffin **10.3g** total fat (**3.2g** saturated fat); **1133kJ** (**271** cal); **37.9g** carbohydrate; **5.8g** protein; **1.5g** fibre

biscuits

mocha cookies

150g butter, softened
¾ cup (165g) firmly packed brown sugar
1 egg yolk
2 teaspoons instant coffee granules
1 tablespoon hot water
1½ cups (225g) plain flour
1 tablespoon cocoa powder
20 dark chocolate Melts

1 Preheat oven to 180°C/160°C fan-forced. Grease and line two oven trays with baking paper.
2 Beat butter, sugar, egg yolk and combined coffee and water in small bowl with electric mixer until smooth. Transfer mixture to large bowl; stir in sifted flour and cocoa, in two batches. Knead dough on floured surface until smooth.
3 Roll level tablespoons of mixture into balls; place 5cm apart on trays, flatten slightly. Press 1 chocolate Melt into centre of each cookie; bake about 12 minutes. Cool cookies on trays.

preparation time **20 minutes**
cooking time **12 minutes** makes **20**
per cookie **7.5g total fat (4.7g saturated fat); 614kJ (147 cal); 18.1g carbohydrate; 1.7g protein; 0.5g fibre**

meringue kisses with raspberry cream

2 egg whites
½ teaspoon white vinegar
½ cup (110g) caster sugar
1 teaspoon icing sugar
raspberry cream
¼ cup (60ml) thickened cream
2 teaspoons icing sugar
1 tablespoon raspberry jam

1 Preheat oven to 120°C/100°C fan-forced. Grease two oven trays; dust with cornflour, shake away excess.
2 Beat egg whites, vinegar and sugar in small bowl with electric mixer about 10 minutes or until sugar is dissolved; fold in icing sugar.
3 Place meringue mixture in piping bag fitted with small plain tube; pipe 3cm rounds, 3cm apart, on trays. Bake about 30 minutes or until crisp and dry. Cool meringues on trays.
4 Meanwhile, make raspberry cream.
5 Sandwich meringues with cream; dust with sifted icing sugar, if desired.
raspberry cream Beat cream and icing sugar in small bowl until firm peaks form; stir in jam.

preparation time 30 minutes
cooking time 30 minutes (plus cooling time) makes 35
per serving 0.6g total fat (0.4g saturated fat); 92kJ
(22 cal); 3.9g carbohydrate; 0.1g protein; 0.1g fibre

choc-peanut cornflakes

395g can sweetened condensed milk
½ cup (140g) crunchy peanut butter
3 cups (120g) cornflakes
80g dark chocolate Melts, melted

1 Preheat oven to 200°C/180°C fan-forced.
2 Combine milk, peanut butter and cornflakes in large bowl. Drop level tablespoons of mixture, 5cm apart, onto two oven trays. Bake about 12 minutes; cool on trays.
3 Drizzle with chocolate; stand at room temperature until chocolate sets.

preparation time **15 minutes (plus standing time)** cooking time **30 minutes** makes **25**
per serving **5.6g total fat (2.3g saturated fat); 577kJ (138 cal); 17.9g carbohydrate; 3.7g protein; 0.8g fibre**

lemon polenta biscuits

250g butter, softened
1 teaspoon vanilla extract
1¼ cups (200g) icing sugar
2 tablespoons finely grated lemon rind
½ cup (85g) polenta
2½ cups (375g) plain flour
1 tablespoon lemon juice

1 Beat butter, extract, icing sugar and 1 teaspoon of the rind in small bowl with electric mixer until combined. Stir in polenta, flour and juice, in two batches.
2 Knead dough on floured surface until smooth. Divide dough in half; shape pieces into two 20cm-long logs. Cover, refrigerate 2 hours or until firm.
3 Preheat oven to 200°C/180°C fan-forced. Lightly grease oven trays.
4 Cut logs into 1cm slices; place, 2cm apart, on two oven trays, sprinkle remaining rind over biscuits. Bake about 15 minutes. Stand 5 minutes; turn onto wire rack to cool.

preparation time **20 minutes (plus refrigeration time)** cooking time **15 minutes** makes **40**
per biscuit **5.3g total fat (3.4g saturated fat); 364kJ (87 cal); 8.4g carbohydrate; 1.2g protein; 0.4g fibre**

glossary

BAY LEAVES aromatic leaves from the bay tree available fresh or dried; has a strong, slightly peppery, flavour.

BICARBONATE OF SODA also known as baking soda.

BLACK-EYED BEANS also known as black-eyed peas or cowpeas; the dried seed of a variant of the snake (or yard-long) bean. Not too dissimilar to white beans in flavour.

BURGHUL also known as bulghur wheat; hulled steamed wheat kernels that, once dried, are crushed into various size grains. Found in most supermarkets. Not the same as cracked wheat.

BUTTERMILK originally the term given to the slightly sour liquid left after butter was churned from cream, today it is commercially made similarly to yogurt. Sold alongside fresh milk products in supermarkets; despite the implication of its name, it is low in fat.

CANNELLINI BEANS small white bean similar in appearance and flavour to great northern, navy and haricot beans.

CAPSICUM also known as pepper or bell pepper. Available as green, yellow, orange, purplish-black and red varieties. Discard seeds and membranes before use.

CELERIAC tuberous root with knobbly brown skin, white flesh and a celery-like flavour. Keep peeled celeriac in acidulated water to prevent it discolouring.

CHEESE
cream also known as Philadelphia or Philly; a soft cow-milk cheese. Also available as a spreadable light cream cheese blend.

fetta Greek in origin; a crumbly textured goat- or sheep-milk cheese having a sharp, salty taste. Ripened and stored in salted whey.
parmesan also known as parmigiano; is a hard, grainy cow-milk cheese. The curd is salted in brine for a month then aged for up to 2 years.
ricotta a soft, sweet, moist, white cow-milk cheese with a low-fat content and a slightly grainy texture. The name roughly translates as "cooked again" and refers to ricotta's manufacture from a whey that is itself a by-product of other cheese making.

CHICKPEAS also called channa, garbanzos or hummus; a sandy-coloured, irregularly round legume. Available canned or dried (the latter need several hours reconstituting in cold water before being used).

CHOCOLATE MELTS, DARK small discs of compounded dark chocolate ideal for melting and moulding.

CHORIZO sausage of Spanish origin, made of coarsely ground pork and highly seasoned with garlic and chilli.

COCOA POWDER also known as unsweetened cocoa; cocoa beans that have been fermented and roasted, then ground into powder.

CORNFLAKES commercially manufactured cereal made of dehydrated then baked crisp flakes of corn. Also available as a finely ground mixture used for coating or crumbing.

CORNFLOUR, WHEATEN also known as cornstarch. Used as a thickening agent in cooking. Also available made from corn.

CURRY
balti paste takes its name from Baltistan, a mountainous region in northern Pakistan; a medium-hot, aromatic paste that contains coriander, fenugreek and mint, which gives it a distinctively mild "green" flavour.
powder a blend of ground spices; consists of some of the following: dried chilli, coriander, cinnamon, cumin, fennel, mace, fenugreek, cardamom and turmeric. Available in mild or hot varieties from most supermarkets.

CUSTARD POWDER instant powder mixture used to make pouring custard; similar to North American instant pudding mixes.

FIVE-SPICE POWDER also known as chinese five-spice. Is usually a fragrant mixture of star anise, ground cinnamon, fennel seeds, sichuan pepper and cloves.

HUMMUS a Middle Eastern salad or dip made from softened dried chickpeas, garlic, lemon juice and tahini (sesame seed paste); can be purchased ready-made from most delicatessens and supermarkets.

LAMINGTON PAN 20cm x 30cm slab cake pan, 3cm deep.

LEEK a member of the onion family. Looks like a large green onion; has a mild flavour.

LENTILS (red, brown, yellow) dried pulses often identified by, and named after, their colour. *French green lentils* are green-blue, tiny lentils with a nutty, earthy flavour and a hardy nature that allows them to be rapidly cooked without disintegrating. They are a local cousin to the famous (and more expensive) French lentils du puy.

LETTUCE
butter has small, round, loosely formed heads with sweet, soft, buttery-textured leaves.
cos also known as romaine lettuce; the traditional caesar salad lettuce. The long leaves have a stiff centre rib that gives a slight cupping effect to the leaf on either side.
green coral very curly and tightly furled leaves that do look like coral; comes in distinctive tasting red and green leaves.

PAPRIKA ground dried red capsicum (bell pepper).

PEARL BARLEY has had the husk removed then been steamed and polished so that only the "pearl" of the original grain remains, much the same as white rice.

POLENTA also known as cornmeal; a flour-like cereal made of dried corn (maize) and sold ground in different textures. Also the name of the dish made from it.

PORK NECK sometimes called pork scotch; a boneless cut from the foreloin.

RICE VERMICELLI also known as sen mee, mei fun or bee hoon. Used throughout Asia in spring rolls and cold salads; made with rice flour instead of mung bean starch. Soak in hot water before use until softened, boil them briefly then rinse with hot water.

RISONI small rice-shaped pasta; very similar to another small pasta, orzo.

ROCKET a peppery green leaf also known as arugula, rugula and rucola. *Baby rocket leaves* are smaller and less peppery.

SEMOLINA coarsely ground flour milled from durum wheat; is the flour used in making gnocchi, pasta and couscous.

SICHUAN PEPPERCORNS also known as szechuan or chinese pepper; native to the Sichuan province of China. A mildly hot spice that comes from the prickly ash tree. Although it is not related to the peppercorn family, small, red-brown sichuan berries look like black peppercorns and have a distinctive peppery-lemon flavour and aroma.

SILVER BEET also known as swiss chard and, incorrectly, spinach; has fleshy stalks and large, dark-green crinkly leaves.

SILVERSIDE also known as topside roast; this is the actual cut used for making corned beef. Cut from the upper leg and cured, it is usually sold cryovac-packed in brine.

SNOW PEAS also called mange tout (eat all). *Snow pea tendrils*, the growing shoots of the plant, are sold by greengrocers. *Snow pea sprouts* are the tender new growths of snow peas.

SPLIT PEAS also known as field peas; green or yellow pulse grown especially for drying and split in half along a centre seam.

SPONGE-FINGER BISCUITS also known as savoy biscuits, lady's fingers or savoiardi; they are Italian-style crisp fingers made from sponge-cake mixture.

SPROUTS also known as bean shoots; tender new growths of assorted beans and seeds germinated for consumption as sprouts. Most readily available are mung bean, soy bean, alfalfa and snow pea sprouts.

SWEETENED CONDENSED MILK a canned milk product consisting of milk with more than half the water content removed; the remaining milk is sweetened with sugar.

SUGAR
caster also known as superfine or finely granulated table sugar.
icing also known as powdered sugar or confectioners' sugar; pulverised granulated sugar crushed together with a small amount of cornflour.
white coarse, granulated table sugar also known as crystal sugar.

SULTANAS also known as golden raisins; dried seedless white grapes.

TAHINI sesame seed paste available from Middle Eastern food stores; most often used in hummus and baba ghanoush.

TURKISH BREAD also known as pide. Sold in long (about 45cm) flat loaves as well as individual rounds; made from wheat flour and sprinkled with black onion seeds (kalonji).

VANILLA EXTRACT obtained from vanilla beans infused in water; a non-alcoholic version of essence.

WOMOBK also known as chinese cabbage, peking or napa cabbage; the most common cabbage in South-East Asia. Elongated in shape with pale green, crinkly leaves, it can be shredded or chopped and eaten raw, braised, steamed or stir-fried.

ZUCCHINI also known as courgette; small green, yellow or white members of the squash family having edible flowers, which can be stuffed then baked or deep-fried.

conversion chart

measures

One Australian metric measuring cup holds approximately 250ml; one Australian metric tablespoon holds 20ml; one Australian metric teaspoon holds 5ml.

The difference between one country's measuring cups and another's is within a two- or three-teaspoon variance, and will not affect your cooking results. North America, New Zealand and the United Kingdom use a 15ml tablespoon.

All cup and spoon measurements are level. The most accurate way of measuring dry ingredients is to weigh them. When measuring liquids, use a clear glass or plastic jug with the metric markings.

We use large eggs with an average weight of 60g.

dry measures

metric	imperial
15g	½oz
30g	1oz
60g	2oz
90g	3oz
125g	4oz (¼lb)
155g	5oz
185g	6oz
220g	7oz
250g	8oz (½lb)
280g	9oz
315g	10oz
345g	11oz
375g	12oz (¾lb)
410g	13oz
440g	14oz
470g	15oz
500g	16oz (1lb)
750g	24oz (1½lb)
1kg	32oz (2lb)

liquid measures

metric	imperial
30ml	1 fluid oz
60ml	2 fluid oz
100ml	3 fluid oz
125ml	4 fluid oz
150ml	5 fluid oz (¼ pint/1 gill)
190ml	6 fluid oz
250ml	8 fluid oz
300ml	10 fluid oz (½ pint)
500ml	16 fluid oz
600ml	20 fluid oz (1 pint)
1000ml (1 litre)	1¾ pints

length measures

metric	imperial
3mm	⅛in
6mm	¼in
1cm	½in
2cm	¾in
2.5cm	1in
5cm	2in
6cm	2½in
8cm	3in
10cm	4in
13cm	5in
15cm	6in
18cm	7in
20cm	8in
23cm	9in
25cm	10in
28cm	11in
30cm	12in (1ft)

oven temperatures

These oven temperatures are only a guide for conventional ovens. For fan-forced ovens, check the manufacturer's manual.

	°C (Celsius)	°F (Fahrenheit)	Gas Mark
Very slow	120	250	½
Slow	150	275-300	1-2
Moderately slow	160	325	3
Moderate	180	350-375	4-5
Moderately hot	200	400	6
Hot	220	425-450	7-8
Very hot	240	475	9

index

117

ARE YOU MISSING SOME OF THE WORLD'S FAVOURITE COOKBOOKS?

The Australian Women's Weekly Cookbooks are available from bookshops, cook-shops, supermarkets and other stores all over the world. You can also buy direct from the publisher, using the order form below.

TITLE	RRP	QTY	TITLE	RRP	QTY
Asian, Meals in Minutes	£6.99		Indian Cooking Class	£6.99	
Babies & Toddlers Good Food	£6.99		Japanese Cooking Class	£6.99	
Barbecue Meals In Minutes	£6.99		Just For One	£6.99	
Beginners Cooking Class	£6.99		Kids' Birthday Cakes	£6.99	
Beginners Simple Meals	£6.99		Kids Cooking	£6.99	
Beginners Thai	£6.99		Kids' Cooking Step-by-Step	£6.99	
Best Food	£6.99		Lean Food	£6.99	
Best Food Desserts	£6.99		Low-carb, Low-fat	£6.99	
Best Food Fast	£6.99		Low-fat Feasts	£6.99	
Best Food Mains	£6.99		Low-fat Food For Life	£6.99	
Cafe Classics	£6.99		Low-fat Meals in Minutes	£6.99	
Cakes Biscuits & Slices	£6.99		Main Course Salads	£6.99	
Cakes Cooking Class	£6.99		Mexican	£6.99	
Caribbean Cooking	£6.99		Middle Eastern Cooking Class	£6.99	
Casseroles	£6.99		Midweek Meals in Minutes	£6.99	
Casseroles & Slow-Cooked Classics	£6.99		Moroccan & the Foods of North Africa	£6.99	
Cheap Eats	£6.99		Muffins, Scones & Breads	£6.99	
Cheesecakes: baked and chilled	£6.99		New Casseroles	£6.99	
Chicken	£6.99		New Classics	£6.99	
Chicken Meals in Minutes	£6.99		New Curries	£6.99	
Chinese Cooking Class	£6.99		New Finger Food	£6.99	
Christmas Cooking	£6.99		New Salads	£6.99	
Chocolate	£6.99		Party Food and Drink	£6.99	
Cocktails	£6.99		Pasta Meals in Minutes	£6.99	
Cooking for Friends	£6.99		Potatoes	£6.99	
Cupcakes & Fairycakes	£6.99		Salads: Simple, Fast & Fresh	£6.99	
Detox	£6.99		Saucery	£6.99	
Dinner Beef	£6.99		Sauces Salsas & Dressings	£6.99	
Dinner Lamb	£6.99		Sensational Stir-Fries	£6.99	
Dinner Seafood	£6.99		Slim	£6.99	
Easy Curry	£6.99		Stir-fry	£6.99	
Easy Spanish-Style	£6.99		Superfoods for Exam Success	£6.99	
Essential Soup	£6.99		Sweet Old Fashioned Favourites	£6.99	
Foods That Fight Back	£6.99		Tapas Mezze Antipasto & other bites	£6.99	
French Food, New	£6.99		Thai Cooking Class	£6.99	
Fresh Food Fast	£6.99		Traditional Italian	£6.99	
Fresh Food for Babies & Toddlers	£6.99		Vegetarian Meals in Minutes	£6.99	
Good Food Fast	£6.99		Vegie Food	£6.99	
Great Lamb Cookbook	£6.99		Wicked Sweet Indulgences	£6.99	
Greek Cooking Class	£6.99		Wok, Meals in Minutes	£6.99	
Grills	£6.99				
Healthy Heart Cookbook	£6.99		TOTAL COST:	£	

To order: Mail or fax – photocopy or complete the order form above, and send your credit card details or cheque payable to: Australian Consolidated Press (UK), Moulton Park Business Centre, Red House Road, Moulton Park, Northampton NN3 6AQ, phone (+44) (0) 1604 497531 fax (+44) (0) 1604 497533, e-mail books@acpuk.com or order online at www.acpuk.com

Non-UK residents: We accept the credit cards listed on the coupon, or cheques, drafts or International Money Orders payable in sterling and drawn on a UK bank. Credit card charges are at the exchange rate current at the time of payment.

Postage and packing UK: Add £1.00 per order plus 50p per book.

Postage and packing overseas: Add £2.00 per order plus £1.00 per book. All pricing current at time of going to press and subject to change/availability.

Offer ends 31.12.2007

Mr/Mrs/Ms _____

Address _____

_____ Postcode _____

Day time phone _____ Email* (optional) _____

I enclose my cheque/money order for £ _____

or please charge £ _____

to my:　☐ Access　☐ Mastercard　☐ Visa ___　☐ Diners Club

PLEASE NOTE: WE DO NOT ACCEPT SWITCH OR ELECTRON CARDS

Card number ☐☐☐☐ ☐☐☐☐ ☐☐☐☐ ☐☐☐☐

Expiry date _____ 3 digit security code *(found on reverse of card)* _____

Cardholder's name_____ Signature _____

* By including your email address, you consent to receipt of any email regarding this magazine, and other emails which inform you of ACP's other publications, products, services and events, and to promote third party goods and services you may be interested in.

If you like this cookbook, you'll love these...

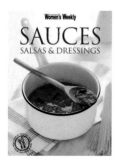
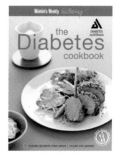

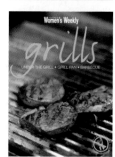

These are just a small selection of titles available in
The Australian Women's Weekly range on sale at selected
newsagents, supermarkets or online at www.acpbooks.com.au

also available in bookstores...

TEST KITCHEN
Food director Pamela Clark
Food editor Karen Hammial
Assistant food editor Sarah Schwikkard
Test Kitchen manager Cathie Lonnie
Senior home economist Elizabeth Macri
Home economists Ariarne Bradshaw,
Belinda Farlow, Miranda Farr, Nicole Jennings,
Angela Muscat, Rebecca Squadrito,
Kellie Thomas, Mary Wills
Nutritional information Belinda Farlow

ACP BOOKS
Editorial director Susan Tomnay
Creative director & designer Hieu Chi Nguyen
Senior editor Wendy Bryant

Director of sales Brian Cearnes
Marketing manager Bridget Cody
Production manager Cedric Taylor

Chief executive officer Ian Law
Group publisher Pat Ingram
General manager Christine Whiston
Editorial director (WW) Deborah Thomas

RIGHTS ENQUIRIES
Laura Bamford Director ACP Books
lbamford@acpuk.com

Produced by ACP Books, Sydney.
Printed by Times Printers Pte Ltd,
16 Tuas Avenue 5, Singapore 639340.
Published by ACP Magazines Ltd,
54 Park St, Sydney; GPO Box 4088,
Sydney, NSW 2001.
phone (02) 9282 8618 fax (02) 9267 9438.
acpbooks@acpmagazines.com.au
www.acpbooks.com.au

To order books, phone 136 116 (within Australia).
Send recipe enquiries to:
recipeenquiries@acpmagazines.com.au

Australia Distributed by Network Services,
phone +61 2 9282 8777 fax +61 2 9264 3278
networkweb@networkservicescompany.com.au
United Kingdom Distributed by Australian
Consolidated Press (UK),
phone (01604) 497 531 fax (01604) 497 533
books@acpuk.com
Canada Distributed by Whitecap Books Ltd,
phone (604) 980 9852 fax (604) 980 8197
customerservice@whitecap.ca
www.whitecap.ca
New Zealand Distributed by Netlink
Distribution Company,
phone (9) 366 9966 ask@ndc.co.nz
South Africa Distributed by PSD Promotions,
phone (27 11) 392 6065/7
fax (27 11) 392 6079/80
orders@psdprom.co.za

Clark, Pamela.
The Australian Women's Weekly cheap eats.
Includes index.
ISBN 978 1 86396 575 0 (pbk).
1. Low budget cookery. 2. Cookery .
I. Clark, Pamela II Title: Australian Women's Weekly
641.552
© ACP Magazines Ltd 2007
ABN 18 053 273 546

The publishers would like to thank the following for
props used in photography: Chee Soon Fitzgerald,
Alfresco Emporium, Village Living, Papaya, Domayne.